Also by Bill Henderson

Tower: Faith, Vertigo, and Amateur Construction

Her Father

His Son

Simple Gifts

ONE MAN'S SEARCH
FOR GRACE

BILL HENDERSON

FREE PRESS

NEW YORK LONDON TORONTO SYDNEY

FREE PRESS
A Division of Simon & Schuster, Inc.
1230 Avenue of the Americas
New York, NY 10020

First Free Press trade paperback edition October 2008

FREE PRESS and colophon are trademarks of Simon & Schuster, Inc.

For information about special discounts for bulk purchases, please contact Simon &
Schuster Special Sales at 1-800-456-6798 or business@simonandschuster.com

Designed by Julie Schroeder

Manufactured in the United States of America

10 9 8 7 6 5 4 3 2 1

The Library of Congress has cataloged the hardcover edition as follows:
Henderson, Bill.
Simple gifts: great hymns: one man's search for grace / Bill Henderson.
   p. cm.
Includes bibliographical references (p.   ) and index.
1. Hymns, English—History and criticism. I. Title.
BV315.H46 2006
264'.23—dc22
2006040771

ISBN-13: 978-0-7432-8473-8
ISBN-10:   0-7432-8473-9
ISBN-13: 978-0-7432-8474-5 (pbk)
ISBN-10:   0-7432-8474-7 (pbk)

Credits will be found on page 191.

For Genie and Lily

CONTENTS

Sing hymns at heaven's gate.

—Shakespeare

Jesus is the poem God made.

—Oscar Wilde

Simple Gifts

Preface

FIRST SONGS

I treasure some of the grand old hymns. My great joy is to sing them with people like me who hold them deep in their memories and call them forth with passion.

At the nondenominational Rockbound Chapel, fastened to a granite boulder on a hill over the sea near Sedgwick, Maine, I sing songs with other summer visitors—strangers and people I barely know. In untrained, inelegant, often too-loud or too-soft voices, we sing to each other of our pain, loneliness, and fear, topics we would hesitate to admit flat out in gatherings after services. We also sing of love, grace, trust, hope, peace—sentiments that are left out of the usual daily patter. We sing words that matter to us.

We are a mixed lot in age, sex, and occupation. We are fishermen, poets, CEOs, clerks, teachers, publishers, builders, mechanics, retirees, holiday rusticators, and others. We sing out our souls for each other. Our hymns are like hugs.

We are Protestants, Catholics, and those who would prefer not to be labeled. Some of us are of troubled faith and others are more agnostic than not. Even if our pew companions don't exactly share creeds, our hymns carry all of us to those Thin Places described by the Irish, elevated states of consciousness where almost all barriers between mortals and gods vanish.

Most of us Rockbound singers, like everybody else, spend portions of our days listening to music on our radios, TVs, or CD players. We are sung at. But in the tiny chapel we find our own voices. It makes no difference how well we sing, only that we do so. We raise our notes to each other and to heaven. No celebrity musician ever receives as much fan-love as we humble amateurs do, from each other, from the spirit within and around us.

My friend Scott Savage, a conservative Quaker, tells me that often hymns "break out." His family's favorite is "The Holy Ghost Is Here," written in 1834 by Charles H. Surgeon. Scott writes: "At the noon prayer before lunch this hymn breaks out, or while we cut up apples for canning applesauce, or on a walk, or returning from meeting, my wife and our two children sing it together unprompted and quite sweetly, while Ned the horse finds his way home."

At the Rockbound Chapel, songs don't break out in quite the same way. We raise our hands before the service and call out the page numbers of cherished songs, while Jim Lufkin, our energetic pastor, scribbles notes and prepares the agenda. After we get rolling, accompanied by a grand older lady, Alice Egland, on the piano—she knows scores of hymns by heart—or with the help of a visiting fiddle, flute, or even a saw player, the spirit breaks out in earnest. In an hour we might cover two dozen hymns, first and last verses, sometimes all the verses. Old, old hymns. Never anything modern.

Words, mere words, flat on the page or preached dead in the air, can ruin faith and often divide congregations. Theological niceties spun by divine theorists for centuries have led to ridiculous and murderous quarrels. Are we saved by grace or works? Does God recognize full-body baptism or a sprinkle? On and on the words of dogma spin into an eternity of nonsense.

As Kierkegaard put it rather bluntly: "When a lark wants to pass gas like an elephant, it has to blow up. In the same way, all scholarly theology must blow up, because it has wanted to be the supreme wisdom instead of remaining what it is, an unassuming triviality."

A great preacher can almost lift mere words into the realm of song, but some don't even come close. Their verbiage leaves me annoyed, bored, betrayed, or asleep. During some sermons in various churches, I daydream that I had brought a basket of ripe fruit to lob at the pulpit. Why should I sit here politely listening? I think, gazing out the window at the blowing tree limbs, the rushing clouds, or the tombstones of the blessedly dead.

We forget such sermons as quickly as possible. We also may forget even the words of wonderful sermons. But hymns—the classic, lasting hymns—resonate from childhood on. Even those of us who haven't warmed a pew in decades can recall hymns we learned in Sunday School, and in such songs our childhood faith is often restored.

William James observes in *The Varieties of Religious Experience* (1902): "In mystical literature such self-contradictory phrases as 'dazzling obscurity' 'whispering silence' and 'teeming desert' are continuously met with. They prove that not conceptual speech, but music rather is the element through which we are best spoken to by mystical truth."

Music is transcendent theology. Hildegaard of Bingen, the twelfth-century mystic and composer, took music so seriously that in one of her plays, while the soul and the angels sing, the devil has only a speaking part. Music has been denied him. Because of his unmelodic nature, he can't approach the Thin Places.

Of course, not all hymns take us there. In fact, some hymns propel us in the opposite direction. They leave us lip-syncing the verses, deflated by trivial or sappy tunes and lyrics, Muzak for the well-fed, somnolent mind. For me, a mediocre hymn is as bad as a lousy sermon, because I am expected to participate in the debacle by at least pretending to sing along. I snap shut the hymnal and stand in silence until the last note relieves the congregation.

But oh! When it hits! When a great old hymn reaches way down inside where you live: then the problem is not shall I sing, but can I manage to sing at all. I choke up and stumble over words and notes. Nothing can mean so much as a classic hymn.

Such hymns go to a source in us beyond our control and leave us overwhelmed with joy and recognition. Suddenly, when words and music combine, I see, as in the tremendous line of "Amazing Grace"—"I was blind but now I see." On paper that line may not mean much. In song, it's almost more truth than I can bear to express.

I rediscovered such a wallop when I sorted through my father's possessions after he died. In his cellar workshop I came across records he had made of himself and our family singing together.

I remember my dad as a shy and mostly silent man. He almost never expressed extremes of emotion and reproved his three children for excessive enthusiasm. "Don't gush," Pop would say. He spent most of his evenings quietly in the cellar, after working all day for General Electric. In his workshop he constructed wood and mechanical projects: a wagon for my brother and me (the "Bill/Bob"); a crutch for my mother when she fell and broke her ankle; a snow-blower concocted out of an ancient fruit tree sprayer; and the device that allowed him to create these records.

His forty-five-RPM vinyl discs were scratchy and definitely homemade, but on one my father's passion for hymns was obvious. He both sang and accompanied himself on the piano. The record label said "Francis, 1948":

"TAKE TIME TO BE HOLY"
Take time to be holy
Speak often with God
Find rest in Him always
And feed on His word.

Make friends with God's children
Help those who are weak
Forgetting in nothing
His blessing to seek.

His voice was a determined whisper, as if he was embarrassed to be recording himself, but behind that whisper I felt a need that he couldn't express in any other way. In his reserve and shyness he often found it difficult to "make friends with God's children." Here he almost cries out that he wants to do just that.

In another of Pop's recordings, I heard my mother and me in 1946 singing "Jesus Loves the Little Children":

> Jesus loves the little children
> All the children of the world
> Red and yellow, black and white
> They are precious in His sight.

And "Jesus Loves Me":

> Jesus loves me!
> This I know
> For the Bible tells me so.

On a record dated "Christmas 1950," I tentatively plunked out my nine-year-old's piano version of "O Little Town of Bethlehem" while my mother encouraged me, "Good, Billy, very good," and Pop stood by with his marvelous machine.

In church, in Sunday School, and at home, we sang together. As World War II ended, the nuclear age began, the Cold War descended, and the Korean War erupted, hymns became our everyday certainty. They lifted us above the world and assured the Henderson children that a greater power than all others protected us in love.

At our church, Philadelphia's Oak Park Fourth Presbyterian, I joined the Junior Choir with my younger brother, Bob. At Christmas and Easter we sang for the congregation. My favorite was "Christ Arose":

> Up from the grave he arose
> With a mighty triumph o'er his foes

> He arose a victor
> From the dark domain
> And He lives forever
> With his saints to reign
> He arose! He arose!
> Hallelujah! Christ arose!

I loved the imaginary pyrotechnics. There was Jesus low, very low, in the dark domain (whatever that was), and suddenly up he rushed, like a huge whale from the ocean depths, with a great splash as he surfaced and surged upward to the sky.

Since I was the tallest child, I was positioned on the back row in front of the altar on the highest step. Attired in my black and white robe, I could sing to all in the stone church below me. "He arose!" I shouted from my pinnacle, as the whale jetted to the stars. "He arose!"

In grade school I started trumpet lessons and my brother tackled the trombone. One July we serenaded the Wednesday night singers at our little summer church on the outskirts of Ocean City, New Jersey. I remember the bare plank floors, wooden folding chairs, an out-of-tune piano, and a few dozen of the faithful. Our first-ever recital. Bob and I stood in front of the group as the sun set through the windows and the ocean sighed a block away. "Trust and Obey" was our duet, a rather simple hymn. We had practiced it hard and were quite confident. We hit the first few notes OK, lost our place, and stopped dead with stage fright. Finally, after a long silence, we were politely thanked by the minister, who escorted the comatose boys to their seats next to their parents and younger sister, Ruth. The congregation applauded lightly.

"That's all right," said the minister. "God appreciates the effort."

It would be decades before I tried "Trust and Obey" again, and then it would be in a big city, deep in my cups.

Gradually, as I became a teen, church and its hymns lost interest for me. Girls, sports, and scholastic ranking were more important.

Pop urged, indeed begged, me to attend services with him and Mom, but I refused. I sang no more hymns.

But I continued to practice the trumpet. It was thought by education pundits that music inoculated kids against juvenile delinquency and made them appreciate the finer things. Music was practical. Plus, said the guidance counselors, trumpet-playing would look good on my permanent record. I would appear "well-rounded" for college admissions (well-rounded was a top virtue of the times). Music was a higher-education insurance policy.

I practiced mightily and progressed to first rank in the junior and senior high school brass sections. In eleventh grade I was named drum major of the Lower Merion High School marching band. In a ridiculous two-foot-tall rabbit fur headpiece, a maroon military uniform and cape, and a long shiny baton, I strode duck-footed onto the halftime football field and blasted my whistle at the musicians under my glorious command. We attempted to entertain the uninterested crowd with our squawking of "Semper Fidelis," "The Thunderer," or "Stars and Stripes Forever." Then we fled the field in ragged lines blaring the school fight song.

I was becoming very well-rounded.

With my brother and a few friends I started a dance band—the Continentals. Like thousands of boys then and since, we thought music was the key to fame, fortune, and girls. I figured we'd become as famous as the Paul Whiteman band. But Saturday practice sessions often ended quickly as we took up our real interest—driveway basketball.

We Continentals managed to learn only two songs—"Beat Me Daddy Eight to the Bar" and "You Always Hurt the One You Love." Our first gig was a Methodist teen dance. Our two tunes lasted only a few minutes. We knew no other tunes. That was it for the Continentals. The minister scrambled around for a record player to fill the void.

Our washed-out school music teachers had long ago lost any zeal for their profession. Years of listening to students butcher the classics had worn them down. They never hinted to me, or they had forgotten entirely, how music could revolutionize heart and soul. However, I was told that a knowledge of classical music was important for college.

I borrowed Beethoven's Fifth Symphony from the library. It was one of the few symphonies I had heard of. I lay on the couch, determined to listen carefully and find out what use this music would be to me. At one point, the theme seems to dissolve as if Beethoven is done with it. Then, as any Beethoven lover knows in his gut, it begins again almost imperceptibly and gathers to a roar of affirmation. Here, I was propelled to my feet in ecstasy. So that's what music can be, I suddenly knew again—a glimpse from the hymns of my past.

After college, I taught school for a year, wandered around Europe for a few seasons, and returned home to Main Line, Philadelphia when my father died suddenly. I expected to be drafted into the army at any moment and shipped to Vietnam.

While waiting for the summons from the draft board, I worked as a reporter for the local paper, but my real office was Roach and O'Brien's bar, a concrete-block eyesore on Lancaster Avenue, the great eighteenth-century Conestoga wagon route to the West. Over R&O's a large neon arrow pointed inward. Flat out, with no frills, it announced "BAR."

Here I learned what a bender was—mourning my father, girl-friendless, spiritless, dreading Vietnam. The jukebox serenaded my bar brothers with the top hits, played over and over. Nobody listened. Now and then we looked up at the TV and the latest reports of body counts.

Sometimes on my car radio I would happen upon an evangelist and I'd recognize the rhythm of his sermons and the cry of his songs. I tried to sing but gave up after a few lines.

All I recalled from the church of my childhood was incomprehensible, doctrinal silliness: Life Everlasting, if you believed in Jesus. If not, Eternal Damnation, and that went for billions of people who never had a chance to raise their hands at Billy Graham, Oral Roberts,

Jimmy Swaggart, or Carl McIntire revivals. These billions burned forever, as did their ancestors at that moment. Could you hear their screams, the cries of the children? And that probably went for Catholics, too, and certainly for Jews.

Couldn't we talk about this sadism? I wondered, staring at the bottles behind the bar. How could anybody believe this stuff? But there was nobody to talk to.

"Is this God a moron?" I'd ask a bar buddy, who had no opinion, hadn't thought about it, but probably suspected that I sounded subversive and maybe unpatriotic.

Are all these people who believe in this God morons also? I continued the conversation with myself. My father believed all that. Was he maybe insane?

My mother admitted she had doubts about particular doctrines, but she was sure Pop was in heaven now and that she would join him some day. What was I missing here? I sat there watching the beads of moisture run down my beer mug while the Beatles sang "Michelle Ma Belle" on the jukebox for the umpteenth time that morning.

Couldn't God have just sent flowers to let us know of His love instead of making His son into a bloody sacrificial lamb? I pondered.

Booze, that's where love was. Dependable, warm, fuzzy beer-and-a-bump love.

What a difference it would have made if somebody had walked into that dark, stale room and announced to us, "God loves you, I love you. That's what this religion is really all about. Love. The rest is nonsense. Come sing with us."

But nobody ever did.

However, this God business, I discovered, did have practical uses. Divinity students were excused from the draft. I played the religion angle and applied to Princeton Theological Seminary. But when I showed up for the interview, I was too shaky and hungover to make much sense.

Crozer Theological Seminary, where Martin Luther King, Jr., graduated, admitted me with a scholarship. But I was too far gone to attend. Besides, somebody who believed all that stuff could use the scholarship more than I. I wrote to them that I was sick. They replied that they were sorry about my illness and I was welcome to join them when I got better. Crozer really did seem concerned about me personally, I noticed, rather amazed.

When the letter from the draft board arrived, I reported for my physical. But they didn't want me. My shrink informed them I was insufficiently violent and too drunk to shoot straight.

Somehow, in the years ahead, I didn't kill myself with booze.

Then one night at a party, many years later, I began to sing again. I was working as an editor for a New York publisher and although I hadn't received an invitation to this fancy book party, that didn't stop me from oiling up at a nearby bar and making an entrance.

Far across the crowded room I recognized the evangelist Ruth Carter Stapleton, sister of then-president Jimmy Carter, sitting on the sofa, temporarily alone. She was the author of one of the just-published books being celebrated that night—a biography of her beer-swilling, loose-lipped brother Billy, proprietor of a Plains, Georgia, gas station.

This was a literary crowd. Theodore White, author of *The Making of the President* series, was the other honored author. Everybody seemed to ignore Ruth, as if she were some sort of born-again freak.

Booze-bold, I strode across the room and, without introduction, plunked myself down hard next to her. Too carefully, I placed my glass on the coffee table in front of us.

"Hi! I'm Bill Henderson," I announced.

"Ruth Stapleton," she smiled.

"I know. I know who you are. You're the only evangelist I've seen for real in person since Billy Graham. Ocean City, New Jersey, 1948. He was in a hall by the boardwalk and you could hear the ocean breaking outside. My dad took me there. He was very religious, believed in faith healing. Billy Graham was just a kid, almost, and very popular. My dad and I sat in the back of the hall and Dad let me sit on the aisle side so I could see straight up to the microphone where Billy spoke."

I stopped for a breath in my rambles.

"Yes?" she smiled, encouraging me.

"You want to hear more?" I stared into her eyes, unsure.

"Certainly."

"My dad was one of the few guys I ever knew who really believed. I mean really, really believed. No doubts. He talked to Jesus all the time. Even on the job. The world around him hardly even existed."

A crowd was pushing out of the dining area and some of the diners came our way.

I found I was holding Ruth's hand. I didn't care what the others thought.

She tightened her grip on my hand, so that I wouldn't pull away. "Tell me more about your dad."

"It seemed like we were the good guys, my dad and I and Billy Graham. I'd heard of the communists but I was only seven years old so I didn't know what all that was, except it was evil. And we were good, and if I looked up I might see Jesus and His angels riding like cowboys across the clouds. Our guys!"

I held her hand tighter. "All those summers in Ocean City, my mom and dad took us to church twice on Sunday, morning and evening. All summer long we sang."

I gazed into Ruth's eyes and began to sing: "Trust and obey, for there's no other way . . ."

She joined me.

In the midst of that clever mob, we sang:

> Trust and obey
> For there's no other way
> To be happy in Jesus
> But to trust and obey.

Nobody paid any attention to us. When we stopped singing, I teared up and couldn't remember the rest of the hymn. I had no more words for her. I leaned over and kissed her on the lips.

Then I knew I was terribly, dangerously drunk and I had to get out of there fast, hopefully without crashing headfirst through the glass table in front of us.

" 'Bye," I managed, and lurched to my feet. I loped through the literati and stumbled down the steps onto the street. Three words began to rearrange themselves in my mind: "If Ruth's God is love, then love is God."

I played with the words. And what is sin? Sin is the withholding of love from others, from yourself, and from God. That's sin. It really had nothing to do with hell and damnation and the only Son of God and the Trinity and all that. This was about love. I was finally beginning to see. And I had started to sing again.

Ruth and I wrote each other in the next year; a few letters filled with her kindness and compassion, but too soon she was dead from pancreatic cancer, and I drifted once again.

In the mid-eighties I married Annie. We had a daughter, Holly, and we lived where we still live—in a hamlet on the eastern end of Long Island. Down the road from our house is a small Presbyterian church, no bigger than a country storefront, with an old steeple that slants toward the rear as if about to crash down on the congregation.

To Annie, church was ceremony—songs and stories. She wanted Holly to know these traditions, so she enrolled her in the church Sunday School. But I resisted attending. The idea of walking into a church after decades of absence evoked astonishing dread. Did hell and damnation live there? How annoying that they might try to welcome me back with their Christian grins.

On the night of February 25, 1990, our part of Long Island was entombed by a record blizzard. Not much moved on Sunday morning and the town's plows managed to cut only a narrow lane to the village center past the church.

My usual Sunday morning ritual was a bagel and coffee in bed with the *New York Times*. But outside I could see no *Times* delivered on the mounds of snow.

"We're off to church!" Annie announced.

"You can't drive down there!" I yelled.

"Yes, I can!" she called back.

In seconds I reasoned that I had to get hold of a *Times* to survive my Sunday in good habit and that I could also chauffeur Holly and Annie safely to church. I'd buy the *Times* at the general store, read it there, and pick them up after the service.

But why not go into church, too?

"I'm coming with you!" I hollered to Annie.

Off we spun into the snow.

With Holly and Annie, I walked through the church door into a mostly empty room. The organist was snowed in. Only a dozen people who lived nearby had turned out. The minister carried us in song. Simple, tentative voices muffled by the snow on the roof. Outside it was silent—not a car, not a crow. We could have been in the Roman catacombs at the very start of it all. No organ propelled us, no piano. We sang as best we could, missing words, mashing notes, but confessing everything to each other in our unadorned voices, as the snow swirled around us.

I don't remember what hymn it was, but suddenly I was gasping for breath, overwhelmed by recognition. In our singing was the love I sought, as we all did. I knew then it was all right for me to be in this little building. Because of that song, and because of my daughter, Holly, singing next to me in her innocence and simplicity, I was back in the church of my father and mother.

Six months later I was a member of the church, and years later I was asked to be an elder and accepted—a cranky, suspicious-of-cheap-doctrine elder, amazed by my title.

The forgotten hymn has brought me full circle.

What follows is my celebration of classic hymns that have sustained me over the years, and more recently have given me hope—even joy—after a diagnosis of serious illness.

There are hundreds of songs that I might have included here, but, as I said at the start, I particularly want to appreciate hymns that I consider to be world hymns—that do not insist on narrow theologies, but rather love, wonder, and simplicity, my names for God.

I

A Brief History of Hymns

M usic has been with us since we slithered from the sea and began to squeak and howl. In fact, if the songs of sea creatures are any indication of our past, our ancestors sang even before they hit the beach. The tunes may be different, but the impulse is the same—to call out in pain, joy, warning, herd fellowship.

The history of early music is fragmentary at best. From a small portion of Greek papyrus or pottery, and even a gravestone, we know that music was everywhere in ancient Greece. Music was thought to heighten the expressive meaning of words, to heal the sick, to change human nature. To the Greeks, music was of divine origin and a microcosm of the cosmos.

Early Christian music was a mixture of pagan, Jewish, and Eastern heritage. But such music was also at the center of nonreligious festivals, and about the time of Pope Gregory (540–604 CE), the church fathers decided to rid sacred music of secular influences. Instruments were forbidden. Plain chant, known now also as Gregorian chant—monophonic, unadorned, and unaccompanied—was sung at prayers and services by monks and priests, but never at Mass by the people. This was music for God only. It had no beat that might encourage hip-swiveling or toe-tapping.

Not until the year 1000 were instruments allowed back in the church, and gradually, over the centuries, music became polyphonic and more complex.

In the sixteenth century, Martin Luther not only changed the church, he also revolutionized sacred music. Luther advocated singing in the vernacular, not in Latin, and he insisted on the participation of the entire congregation in prayer, praise, and music, not just chanting monks and priests. In 1524 he wrote his first hymn, "Dear Christians, One and All Rejoice," to be followed by many others, including "A Mighty Fortress Is Our God." He asked others to compose simple tunes to be sung by his congregations.

Luther stated, "I have no use for cranks who despise music, because it is a gift of God. Music drives away the Devil and makes people gay; they forget thereby all wrath, unchastity, arrogance, and the like. Next after theology I give to music the highest place and the greatest honor . . . experience proves that next to the Word of God only music deserves to be extolled as the mistress and governess of the feelings of the human heart."

He was enraged when church members wouldn't learn hymns or sing them with gusto. For Luther, the new songs—often based on popular tunes or folk music and employing biblical narrative and Psalms—were the marching music of the Reformed church.

When the Puritans arrived in North America in 1640, they soon published the colony's first hymnal, *The Bay Psalm Book,* a collection of psalms sung to simple notes. In 1719, Benjamin Franklin published an edition of Isaac Watts's *Psalter,* imported from England.

Watts is regarded as the founder of English hymnody. Before Watts, only psalms were regarded as suitable for English congregational singing. Watts said he wanted to write songs that used "the common sense and language of a Christian."

Many of the grand old hymns I sang in church as a child, and my mother and father sang in their youth, emerged from eighteenth-century evangelicalism, particularly the compositions of Charles Wesley, including the songs "Christ the Lord Is Risen Today"; "Hark the Herald Angels Sing"; "Love Divine, All Loves Excelling"; and "Jesus, Lover of My Soul."

Another hymn of the time, Augustus Montague Toplady's "Rock of Ages," published in 1776, is one of the most reprinted hymns in American Protestant history, despite or because of its startling imagery:

> Rock of ages, cleft for me
> Let me hide myself in Thee.

The number-one Protestant hymn of all time is "All Hail the Power of Jesus' Name"—sometimes called the "National Anthem of Christendom"—written by a young English minister, Edward Perronet, and published in 1779:

> All hail the pow'r of Jesus' name
> Let angels prostrate fall
> Bring forth the royal diadem
> And crown Him Lord of all!

Wesley's and Perronet's hymns and those of John Newton, Anne Steele, and William Cowper mark the first great outpouring of modern hymnody, and this was followed by another in the nineteenth century in both Britain and North America. One author alone, Fanny Crosby, a blind woman from Brooklyn, New York, wrote thousands of hymns in this period, and some of them we still sing:

> Tell me the story of Jesus
> Write on my heart every word.

> Blessed assurance, Jesus is mine!
> Oh what a foretaste of glory divine!

> This is my story, this is my song,
> Praising my savior all the day long.

In the late nineteenth century, yet another wave of new hymns was inspired by the phenomenally popular international crusades of D. L. Moody and his song leader and songwriter, Ira Sankey. (Later, I will consider the incredible history of "Amazing Grace." Moody and Sankey were a major part of that story.)

Outside the white evangelical mainstream, spirituals emerged from African-Americans, both slave and free. Although the lyrics and music of many spirituals are of unknown origin, by the mid-nineteenth century these songs were at the center of African-American religion and sometimes crossed over to white congregations, too, with varying success. While white churches may have preferred the lyrics and rhythms of Martin Luther's "A Mighty Fortress Is Our God," they could also now and then get down with "A Little Talk with Jesus Makes It Right" or Thomas A. Dorsey's "Precious Lord Take My Hand."

There are dozens of hymns that I remember from my boyhood at Philadelphia's Fourth Presbyterian Church and the little chapel in Ocean City, New Jersey. I sang them then because my parents did, and I wanted to please them, and, of course, God, too. To sing was to be good. The passion was obedience. Although I can no longer sing some with uncritical enthusiasm, they all resonate in my memory—hymns like "Fairest Lord Jesus," "I Love to Tell the Story," "Leaning on Jesus," "Bringing in the Sheaves," "Tell Me the Old Old Story," "Standing on the Promises," "Blessed Assurance," "Silent Night," "O God Our Help in Ages Past," "Living for Jesus," "What a Friend We Have in Jesus," "Faith of Our Fathers," "The Church's One Foundation," "Just a Closer Walk with Thee," "In My Heart There Rings a Melody," "Since Jesus Came into My Heart," "Open My Eyes that I May See," "In Christ There Is No East or West," "Love Divine, All Loves Excelling," and many others.

But these classic songs are becoming museum pieces in many

churches today. Congregations are segregating themselves not by denomination but by worship style. It makes little difference if you are a Baptist or a Presbyterian; what matters is what you sing. Some churches can nurture many styles under one roof; others are too small and see their members wandering off to more modern worship forms, often with overhead projectors prompting words for the currently popular songs. Royalties are paid to hymn writers based on the number of projections.

The five-thousand-member Vestavia Hills United Methodist Church near Birmingham, Alabama, is typical of a large church's sheltering of many song styles. The older worshippers arrive at eight-thirty for a traditional service with a small choir, an organ, and standard hymns from the United Methodist hymnal, including works by Watts, Wesley, and Crosby.

Later, a younger, more casually dressed group is accompanied by a guitar or piano in a praise and worship service emphasizing southern gospel standards like "I'll Fly Away" and traditional hymns such as "Great Is Thy Faithfulness" sung in modern style with projected lyrics.

About eleven o'clock the sanctuary refills with a mixed-age group for a traditional service, while nearby in the fellowship hall young adults and kids participate in the "Rock and Roll Church" with amplified guitar, drums, tambourine, and piano in a handclapping potpourri of songs including gospel, rock and roll (the Doobie Brothers' "Jesus Is Just Alright With Me") and contemporary praise and worship standards like Michael Shields's "I Will Call Upon the Lord."

In the evening the various groups assemble again: the old folks first with their traditional hymns and then the Youth Worship, where teenagers are the musicians, singing loud praise choruses and amplified secular pop tunes with rewritten religious lyrics.

When the old folks die, it is quite possible their hymns will go with them. That would be a shame, as these hymns are the bedrock of our religious culture and have served millions of people in times of joy and sorrow. As the critic George Steiner said, "Music is the new literacy of Western Culture." To me, too often we sound illiterate.

All of this busy industry was unheard of fifty years ago. Most churches followed the same hymnals that had been used for years. To change those hymnals might have seemed troubling.

What began to shake up the congregations was the 1960s popularity of folk music, particularly that of Bob Dylan—a fusion of white workers' ballads, African-American blues, and Celtic laments. Some church musicians examined their hymnals and found them lacking, especially in songs emphasizing moral issues of injustice to the poor and minorities. Often, reformers reworked the old hymns. Sydney Carter, a British folk writer, redid the American Shaker tune "Simple Gifts" into his own version, "Lord of the Dance," which I consider later in this book. Others composed hymns about global awareness (Carl P. Daw's "We Marvel at Your Mighty Deeds") or made confessions for Western social sins (Herman Steumpfle's "O God the Wounded Earth Cries Out") or wondered about old doctrines (Dorothy R. Fulton's "Elusive God") or the evils of war (Thomas H. Troger's "Fierce the Force That Curled Cain's Fist").

They also attempted to make the old hymns politically correct, substituting gender-neutral pronouns for masculine terms (God is not a "He," whenever possible). Such revisions often went to absurd, fussy lengths. In William Cowper's classic "O For a Closer Walk with God," the editors of one hymnal worried that "walk" excluded the disabled. So the hymn was fixed: "O For a Closer Bond with God."

But their tweaking of the classics was nothing compared to the rise of hymn revolutionaries who formed garage bands and married Jesus lyrics to the electric rhythms of rock and roll. Their efforts were most unwelcome in the churches of the time, so an underground circuit of Jesus musicians formed and played in parks, coffeehouses, and a few daring churches like Calvary Chapel in Costa Mesa, California.

In 1973, the Maranatha! music company was started. Within a few years its praise and worship music, through skillful marketing programs, had found a home—not only in some churches but on tapes and CDs and on home and automobile radios. Today such music is a multimillion-dollar industry, offering a wide range of recordings, videos, publications, and websites.

The inspiration for praise and worship songs is rock and roll. Often lyrics are imposed on pop songs that formerly concerned romantic longings and backseat antics. While the hymn references of the early sixties may have been traditional church music, today's revolutionaries are more influenced by international pop tunes. While early reformers may have been preachy and didactic, the praise-song composers concentrate on first-person pronouns above all others. These rock-and-rollers for Jesus eagerly use accessible lyrics, steady rhythms, and constant repetitions to make their often self-obsessed points. Since they are backed by huge corporations, the question arises: Is this about God or money?

Because these tunes are often experienced via recordings of all kinds, including MTV-type videos with vistas of sunsets, beaches, and waterfalls, they do not encourage singing in congregations, which, as far as I am concerned, is a major joy of hymns.

When hymns by Isaac Watts, Charles Wesley, and others are replaced with repackaged pop ditties and "Amazing Grace" is rendered to the tune of the Eagles' "I Got a Peaceful Easy Feeling," I get an uneasy, queasy feeling that corporate greed has subverted religious song.

It is important to remember, however, that hymn pablum has always been with us. Most of the songs in any hymnal are of shallow perspective, mere aspirin for hectic lives. I am encouraged that some praise-song bands like Jars of Clay seem committed to the integrity of their beliefs and shun the blandishments of easy cash. In albums like *Much Afraid, Jars of Clay,* and *If I Left the Zoo,* the band's lyrics are anything but saccharine.

Dan Haseltine, a leader and principal lyricist of the young four-man group, criticizes his own business: "The message of Christianity is a hard thing to want to spend time pondering. The fact that we are sinners, that apart from Christ we're nothing, these are things that are not easy to listen to, yet Christian music tries to make whatever is played easy to hear. It's the good-package mentality."

Haseltine, who claims little talent for himself, unlike others in various branches of the ego-swollen pop industry, says, "God is the one who's working, pushing the pen a bit . . . hymns are the closest thing to poetry that I read. I use them as foundation for what I write."

To me, many pop hymns sound like drivel, starting with "Jesus made me higher than I've ever been before," but then I might say the same for many of Fanny Crosby's thousands of efforts or the less-inspired compositions of John Newton.

Only a few contemporary hymns may survive for the centuries to come. This book appreciates the hymns that lasted to reach my father's and mother's ears and voices and through them my own. I hope they will endure for my daughter's children and their children's children.

As will become quickly obvious, I am an amateur in all departments. I have no formal musical training beyond my days of drum major glory, and about the minutiae of academic theology I haven't the foggiest notion.

Here are extensive appreciations of three classic hymns—"Simple Gifts," "Amazing Grace," and "The Prayer of St. Francis." To me they embody the bedrock Christian experience of simplicity, wonder, and love. Around these songs I celebrate dozens of other hymns.

My opinions are personal, cranky, and joyous. If I have left out any of your favorite songs, I ask your forgiveness.

II

Simple Gifts

SONGS OF SIMPLICITY

SIMPLE GIFTS

I sit on the sun porch of my home in the afternoon October sunlight, listening to a CD of Aaron Copland's *Appalachian Spring*, performed by the New York Philharmonic, Leonard Bernstein conducting. Martha Graham's ballet company danced to this music.

Some of *Appalachian Spring*, taken by Copland from the Shaker original of "Simple Gifts," is familiar to millions of people even though they may not know its origin. For the Shakers the lyrics of this song were at the heart of what they believed.

I sit here in the fall light and wonder if it wouldn't be better to stop right here. How could any words I might write convey what this hymn has meant to so many singers over the years? The subject is vast, unknowable. I want to run from the writing. Better I should lie down and nap in the sun. What could I possibly add in appreciation of these words and music? The answer, I suppose, is that I know only my own heart and uncertain voice. So, from my pew to yours, here is why I love this hymn.

"Simple Gifts" is first of all a monumental poem of very few words—seventy-two, to be exact. The Shakers said these words were received from the spirit world near the end of the Shaker Awakening period in the United States in the mid-nineteenth century. "Simple Gifts" is but one of thousands of songs received by "instruments" or mediums during this extraordinary revival.

The Shakers had been in decline. The original English Shakers were dead and many of their converts were old. Dissension, infidelity, and laxness infected many of the communities, especially among the young, who were often adopted from "The World" of unbelievers or were children of parents who had converted years before. They knew nothing of the years in the wilderness and of the abuses that the Shaker founders had endured long ago.

But it was these very children who started the revival called Mother's Work, after Mother Ann Lee, the sect's founder, dead since 1784. A group of girls in the Watervliet, New York, community fell into trances in the summer of 1837 and reported trips to heavenly mansions and conversations with spirits. Word of the phenomenon spread to other Shaker villages and soon visits from angels, doves, Mother Ann, Jesus, God Almighty, and Holy Mother Wisdom (the female half of the divinity) were commonplace. Most of the flood of new songs received in this period—over three thousand songs in the Lebanon, New York, ministry alone—were memorized by the faithful and transmitted to other Shakers.

Daniel W. Patterson, to whom I am indebted for inspiration and insight, in his definitive volume *The Shaker Spiritual*, recounts from Shaker sources one such gift of a song: A young girl who was lying on the floor "some length of time with her hands in motion, sung a beautiful new song and before ten o'clock she sung two more new songs. Soon after this she was taken to the Office being stiff and helpless; after this she sung another new song and by eleven o'clock she come to, so that she was able to go home."

"Simple Gifts," some manuscripts say, was given by a "Negro Spirit" at the Canterbury, Connecticut, community. Whatever the source, it is usually attributed to the singing of Elder Joseph Brackett of Alfred, Maine, in the summer of 1848. One elder reported that

Elder Brackett had "a remarkable and natural gift to sing by which he would fill the whole assembly with the quickening power of God." Another elder reported Brackett singing "Simple Gifts" at a meeting and turning about "with his coat-tails a-flying."

The song survives in fifteen manuscripts and many hymnals and in the memory of the remaining Shakers at Sabbathday Lake, Maine. It is one of the final gift songs received during the Shaker Revival period and as with many songs before it, the lyrics honor the female principles of Shakers: beauty, order, harmony, and the love of the Christ Spirit.

"Simple Gifts" includes many of Christ's visions without the usual clichés that make nonbelievers scoff and the eyes of Sunday singers glaze over with bored familiarity.

The first central word is "gift." I suppose if you were a mainstream theologian you'd translate that as yet another take on "grace," and you might not be far off. "'Tis the gift . . ." from God. But the Shakers did not sing the word "grace" here, perhaps because they felt they lived in a constant, all-enveloping state of grace. A gift is a particular bit of grace. This song is "the gift," and many gifts were received besides that one: visions, words, other songs, and directions on how to live, among them "to be simple."

Simplicity is not a feature of many Sunday morning sermons these days. To the Shakers it meant a childlike simplicity of spirit—a direct, uncluttered, innocent, fully confessed openness based on Jesus' commandment in Matthew 18:3, "Except ye be converted, and become as little children, ye shall not enter into the kingdom of heaven."

Perhaps simplicity is too threatening to us. Many churchgoers are well-heeled, with too much to hide and too many shoes. However, a sort of ersatz simplicity is fashionable in American life. Thoreau has always been a secular saint, the builder of that cabin by the pond that we all run to in spirit when commercial clutter overwhelms us. But, as I discovered on a recent trip to Walden Pond near Concord, Massachusetts, the replica of Thoreau's shack is surrounded by howling highways. Thoreau's small haven is lost in the din, obliterated by commerce, as are his ideals.

Simplicity magazines like *Real Simple* and *Chic Simple* abound. But you can be sure that none of them want our lives to be truly free of stuff, otherwise their advertisers would lack customers and the magazines would fold. Said the publisher of *Real Simple:* "Our reader has way too much on her plate and doesn't want to give any of it up."

The Shakers looked to the simplicity of Jesus. A homeless wanderer who owned nothing, Jesus reminded us to "consider the lilies how they grow: they toil not, they spin not; and I say unto you, that Solomon in all his glory was not arrayed like one of these." He commanded a wealthy supplicant to sell all he had, for, "It is easier for a camel to pass through the eye of a needle than for a rich man to enter into heaven." But the man turned away in sorrow "for he had many possessions."

Much the same sorrow affects the modern hymn singer, myself included, although I keep my clutter to a minimum—some basic clothes, a manual typewriter, a house, a camp in Maine, an ancient Volvo. I hang on to these things.

We see the value of the gift but we can't go all the way there.

The next gift, right after "simplicity" in the lyrics, is the gift "to be free." I suppose some preachers might jump in here with remarks about being "born again." And yes, this Shaker freedom is similar to such an experience: sins lifted, cares gone, salvation obtained. But "born again" is not the phrase here. "To be free" is to be free of artifice, as innocent as a child.

I am reminded of the Beatles' tune about the Fool on the Hill who watches the sun drift through the sky all day—a simple form of worship. Similarly, the Shakers give the Infinite their full, constant attention. This theme of freedom will come up again in other hymns in this book, particularly "The Prayer of St. Francis."

Right away, because the lyrics are so spare, we sing of the third gift: "to come down where you ought to be . . . in the place just right." This gift reminds me of the parable of the prodigal son who has been far away from home. In a distant country he wasted his funds, his body, and his spirit. On his return home to the place "just right," his father is overjoyed to welcome him.

I, too, was far away from my parents' church for a long time and, in a way, I never came back to the same church. Turning and turning, I changed, and the church changed, too, as it often does. If we do not constantly reinterpret, recherish what we believe, we will have no belief worthy of worship.

I was not in a place "just right"—I was in no place at all. Then on that Sunday morning of the blizzard I sang that hymn with the others without organ or piano and suddenly realized where I had landed. "This is who I am!" I practically hollered in my journal.

For a brief period after that a cappella service I could see the Shaker valley of love and delight and from time to time since, especially while singing, I feel I am in that valley—not on a mountaintop, or a beach, but, as the hymn insists, in a valley, a protected place surrounded by hills (and other singers).

What a terrific word—"delight"—and so far not too corrupted by our advertising industry or lifestyle pundits who will rip off a religious word when convenient: kosher hot dogs that answer to a "higher authority," for instance, or Miracle Whip salad dressing. "Delight" carries a sexual connotation, as indeed it might, considering that it is a part of a dance tune, however chaste the dance.

This is not the bump-and-grind variety of delight. Perhaps only the celibate Shakers, dancing together but separated by sex, could ever realize the full spiritual meaning of delight. This dance's sexual tension would never be relieved by a couple's quick trip to the bushes outside the meeting hall. Indeed, the tension of the dance inspired an ecstasy for God alone.

Today it is difficult to appreciate Shaker celibacy. The idea of men and women living together and forbidden to touch (not even a handshake was allowed, and no Shaker woman could sew a button on a man's clothing when he was in said clothing) seems rather outlandish. Saving it all for God—the exuberant bliss of divine intercourse—is way uncool. Better we should collect Shaker furniture and forget the rest, especially weird Shaker dancing.

"Simple Gifts" is a dance—a Quick Dance, to be precise. Instructions for that Quick Dance are included in the lyrics: "To bow and to bend," "To turn, turn." A Quick Dance was meant to inspire believers, to get their blood moving, and bring them closer to divine gifts. It was one of many formal exercises that replaced the free-form Pentecostal leapings and shoutings of the original Shakers.

After the death of Mother Ann Lee, the new Shaker leaders, Joseph Meacham, an ex-Baptist minister from Connecticut, and Lucy Wright of western Massachusetts, reorganized the Shaker ministries, services, and especially the dances. Other sects of the frontier revivals expressed themselves physically—the Schismatics, New Lights, Methodists, and Baptist Merry Dancers, for instance—but until the Shakers no one had dared to formalize their ecstasies into "laborings" (so-called because everything the Shakers did, no matter how minor, was a consecrated labor).

For their laborings the Shakers were ridiculed by many in The World. Their services became a spectacle for the Sunday carriage crowd and foreign tourists who packed into meeting houses to ogle segregated men and women shuffling and stepping lively in circles or lines facing a vocal band (no instruments allowed). One English visitor announced: "I could have laughed had I not felt disgusted at such a degradation of rational and immortal beings."

A modern psychologist might observe that the exhausting laborings were a fine cooler of sexual passions. The Shakers put it another way: Dances are "the greatest gift that God ever made known to man for the purification of the soul." They cited biblical passages—David dancing before the Ark, for instance. The believers danced like living sparks. They labored to be near God. And often, during and after their laborings, gifts from heaven arrived.

The tradition of Quick Dancing lasted until 1870, but the Shakers labored, in marches and dances, until 1930. By then their fire had become more restrained, and the membership of their faith had greatly declined.

History has seldom been gentle to the gentle Shakers. The founder of the movement, Ann Lee, was born to a large and poor family in Manchester, England, in 1736. At age eight, she was sent to work in Manchester's textile mills—the "dark, Satanic Mills" described in William Blake's "Jerusalem." (For some reason, the hymn of his poem has become the most popular religious song in England, about which more later.) Schooling was rare for poor children, and Ann never learned to read words or music. She worked on her feet—chairs were not provided for children—twelve hours a day, six days a week. On Sunday, while the mill barons occupied pews at the Church of England, the children returned to the mills to clean machines.

When Ann was in her early twenties, evangelists George White-field and John Wesley preached the idea of more direct communication with the Holy Ghost, outside established church order. Ann joined a small group of ex-Quakers—the Shaking Quakers—who sought emotional union with God through public confession and testimony. Ann's fervor at meetings marked her as a leader of the sect—which, among other beliefs, proclaimed that God was two spirits, one male, the other female, after Genesis: "God created man in his own image . . . male and female created he them." The female messiah was yet to come.

In eighteenth-century England, this was not only unthinkable, it was blasphemous. Women were but an enhanced form of property. Lord Chesterfield noted: "Women should be talked to as below men and above children." Martin Luther had been even more blunt: "God gave women hips so they could sit on them."

At age twenty-six, Ann was told by her father to marry his blacksmith-shop apprentice, Abraham Standerin. With Abraham she had four children. All of them died young. Ann was devastated, insane with grief and guilt. She threw herself into the work of the Shaking Quakers, who were now under constant harassment by the Manchester authorities for their heretical doctrines and noisy services.

Eventually Ann and others were tossed into prison for "profaning the Sabbath." In her cell she received the first of two transforming visions: She witnessed Adam and Eve expelled from the Garden of Eden for their lust. From lust sprang all the other evils—vanity, vulgarity, sloth, jealousy, dishonesty, greed—the vices that had reduced working-class England to drunkenness, debauchery, and despair. Sex was behind it all, Ann saw in her first vision. When she was released, she marched forth fearlessly, condemning the Church of England for "condoning marriage."

Such defiance riled the authorities even more. She was stoned by a mob and, according to legend, her prayers deflected the stones and her attackers left exhausted. Then she was locked in a madhouse. Here she received her second vision: Jesus appeared to her and informed her that she was His anointed successor, the long-awaited Second Coming of the Christ Spirit—the female Jesus.

England was too dangerous for such notions, and America seemed their only hope for survival. On May 19, 1774, with eight others (including her now-celibate husband), she set sail on a rotting and condemned vessel, the *Mariah*, and after a harrowing three-month passage, arrived in New York, where the Revolutionary War was about to explode.

Ann's pacifist sentiments did not please New Yorkers. They marked her for a British spy. Finally, her husband could take no more. He threw himself into rum and the arms of another woman.

Ann and her tiny band fled up the Hudson River to a leased plot of land outside Albany called Niskeyuna, "where the water flows," by the Indians. By now they numbered merely four sisters and six brothers. They knew nothing about survival in the winter woods, and here their story would have ended if it were not for the help of the local Indians, an often fierce band of the Mahican ("Wolf"), who declared that Ann was "The Good Woman." They taught the Shakers how to dry seeds, tap maples, hunt and trap, fish through the ice, and stay alive in below-zero temperatures.

For two years, nobody joined their utopian commune. Alone in the wilderness, they endured only because of Mother Ann's strict discipline and regimen of hard labor and constant worship: "All hands to work, all hearts to God."

Unlike the dour, humorless Puritans, the Shakers' elixir in work and worship was joy. The Second Coming of Jesus was real and here now. Mother Ann was the Christ principle. Each moment was an opportunity for celebration.

The exact wording of much of Ann Lee's teachings is lost. Because she could not read or write, she left no paper doctrine. Followers did not write down her sayings until thirty years after her death, when time had left only a blurred memory. For instance, her idea of her relation to God is reported as "your fellow servant," "the second Eve," "the first elder in the Church," and "the bride of Christ." The popular gossip in The World outside that she was the Second Coming of Christ is, at best, inaccurate. The Christ Spirit arrives in each heart one by one, Ann Lee taught—and that is the true meaning of the Second Coming.

Many accounts remain of the charismatic impact she had on others. One convert remembered that Ann Lee "came singing into the room where I was sitting, and I felt an inward evidence that her singing was the gift and power of God. She came and sat down by my side and put her hand upon my arm. Instantly I felt the power of God flow from her and run through my whole body. I was then convinced beyond a doubt that she had the power of God and that I had received it from her."

Another convert wrote in 1780 that he saw Mother Ann "sitting in a chair, and singing very melodiously, with her hands in motion: and her whole soul and body seemed to be in exercise. I felt, as it were, a stream of divine power and love flow into my soul, and was convinced at once that it came from Heaven."

Another recalled that at the sound of Mother Ann's voice a Pentecostal fire swept the hearts of the congregation and "the room would ring with beautiful songs which no man could learn."

In 1780 millennium fever swept the United States. The Second Coming of Christ was expected any day. To usher in the event, a Baptist revival was staged not far from Niskeyuna. But to the disappointment of hundreds, Jesus did not show up. They left depressed. Two Baptist ministers heard of the tiny Shaker colony nearby and, before heading home, paid Mother Ann a visit. So persuasive was she that the ministers were converted to the Shaker Second Coming vision and returned to their congregations with the good news. Entire families and church groups swore off sex, donated their possessions and fortunes to the Shakers, and set up Shaker communities.

In May 1781, Mother Ann declared it was urgent to bring the Shaker message to The World. She set off with five believers on a New England tour, only to discover that religious freedom often meant freedom for *my* religion but not necessarily *yours*. Her efforts hit a dangerous backlash. When the Shakers refused to take an oath of loyalty to the new country (or to any country) and preached pacifism, cries of treason were added to witchcraft, home-wrecking, and the blasphemy of notions, such as the idea that people did not need Christ's atonement for their sins; they could be restored to God through their moral choices—the first of which is to confess all sins and renounce The World. They didn't need the resurrection of the body either, because the true resurrection was not of the body but of the Spirit, as witnessed by the love and peace of the believers. For the Shakers there never has been a full revelation of God's will—which is to be revealed in a progression through the ages.

For such insults to the dogmas of the day, Mother Ann was again jailed and attacked, once by a mob of men and boys who kidnapped and stripped her to see whether she really was a woman.

Despite such brutality, the Shaker band soldiered on from town to town, singing, always singing, wherever they went—songs of greeting, ritual songs, gift songs, dance songs, and songs of farewell, many of them wordless—teaching their tunes to the people they met.

Most of the Shaker songs from this period—said to number about two hundred—made good use of common secular tunes in words, tongues, or sounds. A 1783 account described a group of Shaker travelers singing, "in what they called an unknown language." Another witness reported they "sang in a mixture of words and unknown sounds of words, in a solemn and melodious tone." (It wasn't until 1815 that Shakers studied the rules of music and wrote what they sang, in shape-notes at first. Musical instruments weren't allowed until after the Civil War.)

The Shakers converted many in The World. How wonderful, the converts must have thought, to know that Jesus had truly returned to Earth both in Mother Ann and in the heart of each person. No need for the male Second Coming vision of bloodbaths and fireworks as predicted in Revelation. Mother Wisdom convinced them that Shaker love, peace, innocence, and simplicity were ample evidence that Christ was among them again.

Although an exhausted Mother Ann died soon after her return to Niskeyuna in 1784 at age forty-eight, her movement continued to expand under new leaders. Just before the Civil War six thousand souls called themselves Shakers in nineteen communities from Maine to Indiana.

Even as the Shakers gained converts, The World increased its harassment. Only a year after Mother Ann's death, a Baptist minister,

TESTIMONIES

OF THE

LIFE, CHARACTER, REVELATIONS AND DOCTRINES

OF

OUR EVER BLESSED MOTHER

ANN LEE,

AND THE ELDERS WITH HER;

THROUGH WHOM THE WORD OF ETERNAL LIFE
WAS OPENED IN THIS DAY OF

CHRIST's SECOND APPEARING:

COLLECTED FROM LIVING WITNESSES,

BY ORDER OF THE MINISTRY,
IN UNION WITH THE CHURCH.

The Lord hath created a new thing in the earth,
A woman shall compass a man.   *JEREMIAH.*

HANCOCK:

PRINTED BY J. TALLCOTT & J. DEMING, JUNR.

———◦❖◦———

1816.

Valentine Rathbun, accused them of being un-American, pro-British, pagan, immoral, and pro-Catholic (because of their celibacy and ritual of confession). Said Reverend Rathbun: "Some sing without words in Indian dialects. Others sing jigs or tunes of their own making, which they call 'new tongues.' While some dance, others jump up and down—all this going on at the same time until the different tunes, the groaning, jumping, dancing, the drumming, laughing, talking, fluttering, shoving and hissing make such a bedlam as only the insane can thrive upon. And Ann Lee calls this the worship of God!"

In 1843, Charles Dickens, who enjoyed the favors of a young mistress, visited the Shakers in Lebanon and said he felt as much warmth for the sect as if they had been so many figureheads of ships: "We walked into a grim room, where several grim hats were hanging on grim pegs and the time was grimly told by a grim clock. . . . Presently there strode into the apartment, a grim old Shaker—a sort of calm goblin."

Over time, it was celibacy, aided by such remarks, and perhaps a decline in their own holy passion that reduced the Shakers' numbers. Without children born to Shaker families, they had to rely on converts and adoptions, which dropped off. By 1909 only one thousand Shakers were left in various colonies; by 1930 just one hundred, and today only five keep the faith alive at the Sabbathday Lake, Maine, ministry.

I visited that settlement recently in late October, only to find it closed to outsiders. One of the surviving Shakers, Brother Wayne, a kindly man in his thirties, told me to come back in the spring. I was a tourist out of season. Sabbathday Lake, I felt, was mostly a museum, not the flame but a flicker.

But such a fire they had once ignited! Mother Ann predicted that it would be rekindled one day. And maybe its day has come again. Where do we find in modern America a similar joy? Joy in each other because the Christ Spirit lives in each of us; joy in work. Most Americans can't wait for the weekend. To the Shakers every job was God's job. That's why we revere their furniture and crafts. The Shakers are credited with more than forty inventions, from the major to the minor: the clothespin, the threshing machine, the apple parer, the pea sheller, and a static electricity generator. The Shakers were the first to make cut building nails, permanent-press clothes, and water-repellent fabric, and the first to market seeds in packets—stuff, but truly useful stuff.

Ann Lee and her Shakers were among our earliest conscientious objectors. By insisting on the male/female nature of God, and the equal rights of women, Ann Lee is also arguably a founder of the women's liberation movement.

The Shaker abhorrence of private property pioneered many future communes. Friedrich Engels, no less, called them "the first people to set up a society on the basis of community of goods in America, indeed in the whole world."

We may recoil at their celibacy dictates. But with half of our marriages ending in divorce, and many other unions merely an unhappy compromise, who can blame Mother Ann, whose own coerced marriage produced only the deaths of her four children, for suggesting that unadulterated love of God is a better bliss?

Some wag once famously remarked, "Christianity is a great idea. Too bad nobody ever tried it." Well, the Shakers did for over two hundred years.

As Thomas Merton said, "After their departure these innocent people who once had been so maligned, came to be regretted, loved and idealized. Too late people recognized the extraordinary importance of the spiritual phenomenon that blossomed in their midst."

While the Shakers have almost gone, their ideas, designs, artifacts, and music, particularly "Simple Gifts," have not. Between eight thousand and ten thousand hymns—some with as many as forty variant forms—are preserved in collections. Shaker music may constitute the largest separate folk music tradition in the United States. Some of the early hymns are based on secular tunes, but because the Shakers were isolated from the rest of society, many are unself-conscious and totally original creations.

After almost two centuries of ridicule, and then decline, the 1930s Depression era witnessed, especially among artists, a revived interest in the Shakers. Doris Humphrey's ballet, *The Shakers* (1931), was inspired by their "directness, meticulous structure, immaculate line devoid of superfluous ornament . . . in the uncluttered rooms of their functional dwellings, in their fastidious dress, in the austerity and practicality of their lives. Yet within these calmly balanced lives dwelt also the passion of religious exaltation and the tension of sexual frustration."

Throughout the 1930s Charles Sheeler painted and photographed Shaker buildings and collected Shaker crafts. During the same years, Edward Andrews published two texts, one on Shaker furniture and another on Shaker songs. It was through Andrews that Aaron Copland discovered "Simple Gifts" and used it in *Appalachian Spring*.

The joining of this tune with the composer and then again with the choreographer, Martha Graham, seemed fated. Copland himself was a warm but reticent and unostentatious man. Even after his music made him rich, he lived simply and gave away much of what he earned to people in need. "Simple Gifts" expresses the man.

Leonard Bernstein said of Copland: "Can you imagine Aaron wearing a ring, a jeweled cufflink? It's unheard of! It goes with *Appalachian Spring* and *Our Town*, which I think of as a self-portrait of Aaron. No conspicuous consumption."

Copland wrote *Appalachian Spring* as a score for Martha Graham in 1943 and 1944. According to Copland, the ballet had no name until just before the premiere. He asked Graham, What should we call this thing? She replied, "Oh, dunno, *Appalachian Spring*"—after a section of Hart Crane's poem "The Dance."

Graham, the daughter of a Pittsburgh Presbyterian minister, was herself a bit of a Shaker. She was described as somewhat prim and restrained, simple and yet strong. She felt deeply about her heritage of New England pioneer stock and American folk roots. In *Appalachian Spring,* she aimed at nothing less than the revelation of a people's soul.

The ballet and Copland's music were instantly popular. Graham's troupe toured all the major cities and brought "Simple Gifts" from total obscurity into national consciousness.

Near the end of "Simple Gifts" is a word that leaps out at me: "Ashamed." "We shan't be ashamed."

I never thought of the Shakers as ashamed, at least in the sense implied here that the surrounding culture thought them odd, and it affected them badly. Their history is one of boldness, indeed even brashness, in proclaiming that the Christ Spirit had returned in Mother Ann. But they, too, were ashamed from time to time, and regretted their shame.

Today, Christians who actually attempt to practice their faith outside Sunday services may also feel embarrassed in a society that worships cash. I think of my devout father, who apparently went through a dark night of the spirit back in the 1920s when he was an engineering student at the University of Pennsylvania. On a scrap of paper tucked into one of his textbooks that I discovered after he died, he wrote: "Be not ashamed. Proclaim Him to all."

I don't think he ever sang "Simple Gifts." It's not in the old Presbyterian hymnals. I know he would have appreciated the song—despite his disapproval of dancing. (He forbade me to attend my sixth-grade dance class.) Pop lived very simply, even austerely. He owned an old Chevy and two suits—one for church, one for work—plus a house and a summer place for his family. His was an undecorated existence. Like the Shakers, he lived for God. As he drove from job site to job site for General Electric, he listened to the evangelists on his car radio predicting the Atomic End soon and the Second Coming of the Prince of Peace.

Some hymnals include a "Simple Gifts" knockoff—"I Danced in the Morning," by Sydney Carter, written in 1963 and grafted onto the Shaker tune. The idea of religious dancing is bright and new here, but it is Jesus alone who does the dancing. "I am the Lord of the Dance, says He." Jesus dances for the scribes and the Pharisees and fishermen and He even dances on the cross. And of course, we should dance as He does, the hymn implies.

This is a rousing hymn, mostly because of the tune, and I responded to it wholeheartedly on first singing, until I sat down in the pew after service and thought about the words. My problem is I don't see Jesus dancing. We dance for Him, not vice versa. I think many hymn singers would be upset if Jesus actually boogied down.

The Jesus of my tradition is a fellow who never cracked a joke, although he seemed to have enjoyed a glass of wine now and then, sometimes of his own making. He dined with prostitutes and tax collectors, to the shocked disapproval of the established religious folks. But He is terribly serious throughout biblical accounts. He is a man with a mission, and when this hymn asks us to watch Him dance, literally or figuratively, I balk.

How stuffy of me, I think.

My favorite spiritual dancer is my daughter, Holly. As a young child, recently arrived from a Wordsworthian heaven and remembering it well, Holly could dance almost as soon as she could walk. Hers was the simple gift of children. Before she knew the custom of clothing, she danced naked interpretations for her mother and me. Holly's preference was Gershwin's *Rhapsody in Blue*—she adored the music with her body. Holly was near the Thin Places, right there with the Shakers.

Holly's dancing was one of her gifts to us. And there are many such gifts in all of our lives that we don't recognize—tiny gifts, every-day hints of grace. We rush past them, blinded in our busyness.

One such hint of grace came to me in an undeniable burst. While selecting the hymns for this book, I had a notion that I, too, might try to create a hymn that summed up all I felt about the divine, a universal hymn. I have no particular musical talent and as to the lyrics, I hadn't a hint: Where to begin? And what could I possibly add to what had been written in hymns over the centuries? I let the notion fade away.

Then, one night when I was in a deep sleep, a song came to me, similar to a Shaker gift. I remember an immense light, a truth beyond words, and a vast choir singing. All certainty had been given to me.

I woke up, determined to write this down. But to do so I would have had to waken my wife next to me and fall over my dog, Lulu, sleeping on the floor by the bed. But why write it down? An experience this overpowering could not be forgotten. At dawn, I'd surely remember the words and the tune and the message.

But at dawn the gift had drifted away. Perhaps there never had been any words and music. Maybe I just dreamed the choir. I was left with only a few lyrics that I attempted to reconstruct as the sun rose:

> It's so easy
> So plain to see
> It's there for you
> It's there for me.

What could this mean? The Shakers would have no problem with the lost words. Mere sounds would have done fine. But I couldn't even recall the sounds. "So plain to see"—What? Love? Wonder? Perhaps I had been directed to see what I already saw, to really know what I already knew: a simple gift.

———

Whenever I hear a work of art and passion such as "Simple Gifts" described as "classic" (as I have done), I shudder a bit. "Classic" usually means admired but seldom viewed, read, or sung.

The themes from "Simple Gifts" are central to more popular hymns. These hymns are often sung in church while "Simple Gifts" stays on the high shelf of ballet and concert hall performance. Three such songs are "He Lives!" (the living Christ); "In the Garden" (religious sensuality); and, among a host of Christmas carols honoring the Shaker idea of childlike innocence and simplicity, Christina Rossetti and Gustav Holst's "In the Bleak Midwinter."

"He Lives!" the great evangelical roof-raiser by Alfred H. Ackley, is an early twentieth-century composition. Here, the joy in Christ's resurrection comes roaring out. Ackley makes palpable Thomas à Kempis's statement: "I choose rather to be a pilgrim upon the earth with thee, than without thee to possess heaven. Where thou art, there is heaven."

When I was a boy, Easter meant hand-painting hardboiled eggs with the other neighborhood kids, waiting for the Easter Bunny on Sunday morning and his basket of chocolates, yellow marshmallow ducks, and bouquets of lilies decorating the dining-room table and the church altar. Spring meant ladies at services with elaborate hats, which they wore without embarrassment, kicking off the inhibitions of winter.

My real joy was not so much the tale of resurrection, which meant little to me, since I knew next to nothing of death as yet, but the whole blooming spring thing, especially baseball. Spring was evening pickup games in the narrow street in front of our house with trees for bases, and a game every morning in the rising sun on the school playground before classes.

Spring was also the return of reptiles from hibernation and my chance to catch Painted Pond turtles, bullfrogs, and water snakes at

HE LIVES

Alfred H. Ackley

Go quickly and tell . . . His disciples that He is risen from the dead.
— Matthew 28:7

ACKLEY
Alfred H. Ackley

1 I serve a ris - en Sav - ior, He's in the world to - day;
2 *In all the world a - round me I see His lov - ing care,*
3 Re - joice, re - joice, O Chris - tian, lift up your voice and sing

1 I know that He is liv - ing, what - ev - er men may say;
2 *And though my heart grows wea - ry I nev - er will de - spair;*
3 E - ter - nal hal - le - lu - jahs to Je - sus Christ the King!

1 I see His hand of mer - cy, I hear His voice of cheer,
2 *I know that He is lead - ing through all the storm- y blast,*
3 The Hope of all who seek Him, the Help of all who find,

1 And just the time I need Him He's al - ways near.
2 *The day of His ap - pear - ing will come at last.*
3 None oth - er is so lov - ing, so good and kind.

He lives, He lives, Christ Je - sus lives to - day!
He lives, He lives,

He walks with me and talks with me a - long life's nar - row way.

He lives, He lives, sal - va - tion to im - part!
He lives, He lives, He lives,

You ask me how I know He lives? He lives with - in my heart.

Smith's Pond. I kept a zoo of my limited turtle catch in a backyard turtle pen. The snakes and frogs lived in a glass aquarium in my room and the basement. Spring was all outdoors, afire and alive for a young boy—until developers plowed under Smith's Pond, smothering all that lived there, and erected a suburban housing development on their graves.

But for Pop, Easter meant that Jesus had indeed conquered death and so would all who believed in Him. Someday we would all be together again as a family in heaven. God fixed that for us, just as He fixed everything in the universe, although His purposes were sometimes mysterious: holocausts, earthquakes, wars, deaths of innocents, tornadoes, that sort of thing, which it was best to forget about, since none of it made any sense. Someday in heaven we would all understand.

Pop was utterly sure of that. He asked few questions of the

Bible, or of himself. He clung to his faith as a drowning man to a log. For him to question deeply was to risk total confusion and perhaps, I have often thought, insanity.

Mom, who wanted no fusses, did not quiz him on particulars of his belief. Only after he died did she admit to me, shockingly, I thought, "Daddy was too religious."

After his funeral she chided herself for her mourning. It was tax time and she sat at the kitchen table among stacks of forms: "I know Daddy's in heaven now and seeing beautiful things, but I'm still here and have to do all the things we used to do together, like figuring out the taxes. And I guess my loneliness is selfish. He's happy. But I can't help it." She, too, had no doubts about eternal life.

And, in my own way, neither do I. That's why I love to belt out this tune of a Sunday on Long Island or at a singing evening in Maine, reserving in my mind a few questions for afterward. "Do you really believe all that resurrection from death, I mean physically up from the grave?" I ask a few congregants, expecting shocked looks in return.

They smile, and have not yet thrown me out of the congregation. Maybe something like this will happen, they imply. We all have doubts . . . and hopes.

But now and then, a visiting minister of the moment—we have had several over the past decade—might flat out declare: "If you do not believe He came back from the dead in a real body, you are not a Christian. This is the key to what we believe. Without the physical resurrection, we are nothing."

And so I muse about that real-body stuff, dismiss it, and sing this hymn with even more fervor. "He lives!" we shout. "You ask me how I know He lives? He lives within my heart!"

Surely this is one of the great finales to any hymn—defiance against doubters, a rollicking cheerleader's tune rising up with the last notes; a yelp of utter affirmation. Jesus is irrefutably alive—in our hearts.

That is the Shaker idea, and mine, too.

After lunch with Rick Moody, a young writer who has been up and down and seen about every side of life firsthand, I was talking religion. We walked on New York's Park Avenue South, a busy four-lane boulevard. Rick agreed with my own theory of resurrection: "He's here now, all around us! Why don't church people see that? Why wait for the Second Coming? Why wait for heaven?" And with that, he stepped into traffic and I had to block his way with my arm before he risked his own life with such happiness.

"He Lives!" celebrates that joy. Love surrounds us every second, if we'd only have faith, only see.

"He walks with me and talks with me . . ." (Hit the "walks" and "talks" hard when you sing.) Of course, if you were to walk down a street like my friend Rick, walking and talking to Jesus, you might be carted away for disturbing the peace, as were Mother Ann and the other Shakers. So we keep these chats quiet, as my father did, while we go about our mundane jobs. We wish we could testify, but that might cause a commotion. Best this is a silent walking and talking.

But if you conceive of Jesus as I do, that is a sad private conversation. Nobody should fear the light of love demonstrated and spoken. It's only the born-again, Jesus-is-coming-soon, hell-awaits-the-unsaved, self-satisfied proselytizers toting their placards or thumping their floppy texts on TV that put us off.

"He Lives!" with its insistence on the nearness of Jesus, gets it right—especially with its mention of need. "Just the time I need Him, He's always near." Without need, most of us have little use for Jesus.

Of course our secular society is convinced it has solved the matter of need. Of what use is Jesus—a problematical historical fellow at best—when we have real *People* gods, new ones every month, touchable by way of our TV screens. Celebrities are not the stuff of faith in the unseen. They are here—and soon gone—divinities of the moment.

And they love you, too. See how they smile, how they need you to view their most recent product at the theater. They hunger for your applause, your laughter, your box-office votes.

Need? If you lack for sex, check out the Internet. In the privacy of your own home you can enjoy all the solo sex you want. If you lack for peace, pop a Prozac or an Ecstasy pill. Money? Banks are eager to send you a credit card at loan-shark rates. Food? There's plenty for all; too much. What need do you have that a secular society couldn't fill?

But we all know that the Shakers were right. No matter how filled our porn libraries, our medicine cabinets, our wallets, or our refrigerators, commercial placebos leave us, at best, only quietly desperate. This is a desperation we admit to only in sudden moments of crisis. The need is always there, and only that living love we find in each other and in walking and talking with the spirit of Jesus can fill it.

The composer of "He Lives!" words and music, too, Alfred H. Ackley, was born in 1887 and died in 1960, which makes him more of a modern composer than many others in this book. His hymn first appeared in *Triumphant Service Songs* in 1933, and reportedly was inspired by his attempts to convert a young Jewish student who had been attending evangelistic meetings conducted by Ackley. I am bemused by the idea of a Christian trying to convert a Jew. Christianity is, after all, a later branch of Judaism. What's to convert?

"Why should I worship a dead Jew?" asked the student.

"He lives! I tell you. He is not dead, but lives here and now! Jesus Christ is more alive today than ever before. I can prove it by my own experience, as well as the testimony of countless thousands," Ackley is said to have replied.

And he sat down at the piano and created "He Lives!" in a fit of inspiration. The reaction of the would-be convert to his exclamations is not known.

Perhaps the second verse of this hymn gave the student second thoughts. The lyrics are tired and full of clichés: "My heart grows weary" and "stormy blast," for instance. And the rhymes are embarassing: care/despair and blast/last. Is Jesus coming "at last" stuck on only to rhyme with "blast"? Probably not, but it almost seems that the theology follows the rhyme scheme, and not vice versa.

The real question is, of course, why would you insist that Jesus come "at last" when He is right beside you at every moment anyway?

For the Second Coming, of course. Actually, it's the Third Coming, if you count the birth and then the resurrection and the predicted third appearance. But let's not get stuck on mathematical niceties. What bothers me here is the physicality of all this. Why do we want Jesus in the flesh? What if He shows up with a nose ring? What if His hair really is as long as in the usual Jesus portraits? What if He has a tattoo that says "Mother"? What if He's gay, bisexual, or nonsexual? What if He's a Wall Street WASP? What if He's dumpy, bald, or black?

I saw such a divinity once in high school and that's what he was, not so handsome. His name was Father Divine and he ran a church in Philadelphia with his wife, Mother Divine. Father Divine was black and old; his wife was young and white. His congregation was of all races and ages, and they adored him.

In 1958, I visited Father Divine's church to write a high school class paper on him and his movement, which was very popular and politically significant in the Philadelphia of the 1950s. His followers numbered in the many thousands.

Food was free at the Divine church, and I sat down in a large hall with dozens of people at many rows of tables. We were fed well; heaps of mashed potatoes, chicken, and vegetables. We sat and waited for God to appear. Father Divine kept us waiting.

Finally, to a standing ovation, he entered the room with Mother Divine right behind him, and simply sat down and smiled. Said nothing. Never opened his mouth or said a word. Mother Divine did the same. They didn't eat. They didn't preach. They allowed themselves to be adored.

Father Divine was short, bald, and dumpy, dressed in a too-tight sports jacket and about as plain a fellow as you could imagine. But he said he was God, and many believed him. To his followers, his physical appearance, including his race, meant nothing whatsoever, even as Mother Divine's sex and color were of little consequence to her flock.

To me, a seventeen-year-old recent convert to philosophy (Nietzsche, Schopenhauer, and so forth), he was of interest only as the subject of a senior paper. Do any of us really want to see the physical Jesus? What sort of curiosity is this? Does it make any difference whatsoever that Jesus becomes flesh yet again? Isn't it of far more significance that He live with us every day as the unconditional love that we know He is?

The second verse of "He Lives!" bothers me in another way. Why is it that every Easter we endure this orgy of reconstructed flesh? Isn't this the exact opposite of common dogma? The body is the problem, we are told. The sins of the flesh; the flesh is weak; the way of all flesh; the fleshpots of Egypt—on and on. What we really long for from each other—friends, husbands, wives, strangers—is the spirit of the person in front of us. We want to touch that spirit and be touched in return.

But it's not just Jesus' physical Second Coming that this lackluster second verse reintroduces into this astonishing song. The verse also, of course, reminds us of the full agenda for this event: the Judgment of the quick and the dead. Wow! Such lovely self-satisfied dreams of vengeance (under the guise of "justice") flit into the hymn singer's mind at this point. Dreams of Revelation:

> Then from the sanctuary I heard a loud voice, and it said to the seven angels, "Go forth and pour out the seven bowls of God's wrath on the earth."
>
> So the first angel went and poured his bowl on the earth; and foul malignant sores appeared on those men that wore the mark of the beast and worshipped its image.
>
> The second angel went and poured his bowl on the sea and it turned to blood like the blood from a corpse; and every living thing in the sea died.

And so forth.

Thus, Jesus is said to return. The Second Coming will not be a great day for loving kindness, at least according to Ackley's second verse.

Thankfully, we are immediately into the refrain and on to the third and final verse, which quickly obliterates the tired nonsense of verse two: "Rejoice . . . Lift up your voice and sing."

Yes! And we soar through "eternal hallelujahs" to the bucket-thumping "The Hope of all who see Him/The Help of all who find." (Hit the words "hope" and "help" really hard.) What a great line! I could not argue with this. What is this hope and help? The hymn answers: the spirit that is "so loving, so good and kind."

Every person alive longs for just that spirit although their longings may be buried deep in bitterness and depression. This hope and help is the pearl of this religion. The hymn offers the irrefutable argument for heaven on earth, right here, right now. "He lives within my heart!"

In this idea the Shakers and Ackley are not far from John Lennon's dreaming in his contemporary secular hymn "Imagine." Imagine people, living just for today. No possessions, no nations, no religions to divide us.

Lennon's dream is Jesus' dream. We are all children of the same Spirit. Jesus' great commandment is honored in Lennon's hymn: "Love the Lord your God with your whole heart, soul and mind and love your neighbor as you love yourself." That's all you need to know. Tomes of unnecessary theological ponderings have been written about Jesus. For me it all comes down to that simple vision.

Lennon believed that heaven and hell are here and now. You don't wait for them. Love walks among us. We don't have to save up virtues like a bank account for the hereafter, or win merit badges for regular church attendance. Living for each other today is all that's required.

Lennon's "Imagine" has had enormous worldwide impact. He

once said, "The Beatles are more popular than Jesus," and for this he received death threats. In that murderous reaction and in the actions and propaganda and lies of the organized Church through the ages, you can marshal reams of arguments against this religion. Perhaps Jesus never existed, He's made up; the Gospels contradict themselves; the Bible is a mixmaster brew of sex, violence, wishful thinking, and outright fabrications. The God of this very human anthology is often depicted as both cruel and insane. He begins as a horrid, revengeful, foolish adolescent, the kind of boy who likes to pull the wings off butterflies. He drowns His entire creation in the Flood in the first-ever genocide. He evolves to a God of forgiving love, and then, in Revelation, reverts to a fellow Saddam Hussein would appreciate, yowling about rivers of blood and slaughtered infidels and mumbo jumbo about seven angels.

If that's not evidence enough about the bankruptcy of some established churches, you might bring up the hideous crimes of official Christianity through two thousand years: the Crusades, the Inquisition, the endless religious wars that persist to this day, the institutional anti-Semitism that readied Europe for the Holocaust, and a persistent denigration of African-Americans, Native Americans, and women.

You can say all of this against this religion—and I'd understand—but what I cannot deny is what lives. This Jesus, this love does live and this hymn gets it just about right.

The dancing Shakers—in the name of celibacy—cultivated an explosive sexuality. Strict chastity is a potent aphrodisiac. The tension of denial must explode somehow.

For me, the most sensual hymn in the hymnal is "In the Garden." The hymn is a sort of concentrated Song of Solomon, but for an unannounced reason, this gentle and lovely poem has been abruptly dropped from the new Presbyterian hymnal. Too sexy perhaps.

IN THE GARDEN

C. A. M.

C. Austin Miles

1. I come to the gar-den a - lone, While the dew is still on the
2. He speaks, and the sound of His voice Is so sweet the birds hush their
3. I'd stay in the gar-den with Him Tho' the night a-round me be

ros - es; And the voice I hear, Fall-ing on my ear; The
sing - ing, And the mel - o - dy That He gave to me, With-
fall - ing, But He bids me go; Thru the voice of woe, His

CHORUS

Son of God dis - clos - es.
in my heart is ring - ing. And He walks with me, and He
voice to me is call - ing.

talks with me, And He tells me I am His own, And the

joy we share as we tar - ry there, None oth-er has ev - er known.

You can attempt to sing it on the sensual level only and howl at the deaf, repressed, hypocritical Christians, or you can see another level; in fact, several other levels: an incredible sweetness of imagery—the dew on the roses line is perhaps one of the best ever penned; a precise description of sound—a voice so sweet that the birds "hush their singing" to listen; a melody that rings constantly in the singer's memory.

Yet another level is the sound of the voices here—two voices really, the one that falls on the ear and the "voice of woe," disembodied voices that carry the sound of Jesus' own words, particularly in verse two and the ecstatic refrain, "And He walks with me, and He talks with me." This is a rhythm to walk around with all day in a world that often regards you as dispensable traffic.

But the real defense of the hymn is the quite special picture that writer/composer C. Austin Miles had in mind when he created "In the Garden" in one day.

It is the story of Mary Magdalene's moments with the risen Christ. I have read the Gospel of John's evocation of this scene many times, and always with gasps of sorrow, joy, and recognition. If you accept John's account as a metaphor for the gospel's rebirth or as a literal retelling of the Savior's resurrection, then this narrative is convincing.

While it was still dark, the other disciples have come, seen the empty tomb, and left, crushed in spirit. Mary was His loyal disciple and apparently the only one with courage enough to stay at the tomb. She was a resident of Magdala on the southwest coast of the Sea of Galilee, and Jesus was said to have cast seven devils out of her—a faith-healing I accept, having suffered from various lesser devils myself. Perhaps Mary had nowhere else to go.

Mary remains alone, weeping, outside. When she stoops again to look into the sepulcher, she finds two angels there, dressed in white. According to the New English Bible:

"They said to her, 'Why are you weeping?'

"She answered, 'They have taken my Lord away, and I do not know where they have laid Him.'

"With these words she turned around and saw Jesus standing there, but did not recognize Him.

"Jesus said to her, 'Why are you weeping? Who is it you are looking for?'

"Thinking it was the gardener, she said, 'If it is you, sir, who removed Him, tell me where you have laid Him, and I will take Him away.'

"Jesus said, 'Mary!'

"She turned to Him and said, 'Rabboni!'"

Even typing this, I shudder at the joy of this meeting. Here, encapsulated, is the essence of Mary and of our longing for people lost to us in death, and for an immortality for all of us. And, for Mary, we sing out, after two thousand years, feeling her happiness.

Jesus reveals Himself to her—in spirit, in body (I don't think it makes much difference)—and Mary's ecstasy follows. In this the hymn is utterly correct: No other human being has ever known this sensual joy. He is alive again! I can barely write the words. This hymn is an attempt to describe an event beyond any other.

C. Austin Miles leaves us this account of the hymn's creation:

One day in April 1912, I was seated in the dark room, where I kept my photographic equipment and organ. I drew my Bible toward me; it opened at my favorite chapter, John 20—whether by chance or inspiration let each reader decide. That meeting of Jesus and Mary had lost none of its power and charm. . . . My hands were resting on the Bible while I stared at the light blue wall. As the light faded, I seemed to be standing at the entrance of a garden, looking down a gently winding path, shaded by olive branches. A woman in white, with head bowed, hand clasping her throat, as if to choke back her sobs, walked slowly into the shadows. It was Mary. . . . She saw Jesus standing. So did I. I knew it was He. She knelt before Him, with arms outstretched and looking into His face, cried, "Rabboni!" I awakened in sunlight, gripping the Bible, with muscles tense and nerves vibrating. Under the inspiration of this vision I wrote as quickly as the words could be formed the poem exactly as it has since appeared. That same evening I wrote the music.

Personally, I have known of the sensuality hidden in and inspiring our faith.

My first wife, Nancy, who was a young nun before she entered Bryn Mawr College, quit her order, and shortly afterward, met me.

Her first marriage was with Jesus. She was called Sister Dolores (a sister of dolors and sorrows), before she broke it off after five years.

Her marriage to me wasn't much longer—seven years—but we met at a critical time for both of us. We had both lost our religious vision, and, appropriately, met on bar stools at Roach & O'Brien's bar.

Nancy left behind a sensual, detailed, and now-out-of-print account of her convent life, *Out of the Curtained World* (Doubleday, 1971), which reminds me in sections of the sensuality of "In the Garden."

She poignantly recalls her years as a novice and the lovely, innocent passion of her first wedding day:

The Church-Bride of Christ spoke of her Bridegroom in the Canticles. I said in my heart with the Church, "Let him kiss me with kisses of his mouth! More delightful is your love than wine! Your name spoke is a spreading perfume—that is why the maidens love you. Draw me!"

"Draw me," I prayed.

I thrilled to think of Christ saying about me as well as

about His Mother and the Church: "As a lily among thorns, so is my beloved among women."

And we brides answered, "As an apple tree among the trees of the woods, so is my lover among men. I delight to rest in his shadow, and his fruit is sweet to my mouth. . . . My lover is radiant and ruddy; he stands out among thousands. His head is pure gold; his locks are palm fronds, black as the raven. . . .

"Be swift, my lover, like a gazelle or a young stag on the mountains of spices," I quoted in prayer as we followed our mistress down the wide staircase.

We walked toward a large parlor, where a temporary altar in white satin, white gladioli, and brass had been set up, bordered by potted palms. The other sisters and our families sat in lines of chairs.

The bishop stood in gold cope and miter before the altar. He turned to address us, the brides. "Hear, O daughter, and see; turn your ear, and forget your people and your father's house. So shall the king desire your beauty; for he is your lord. . . ."

Mother Benedict took me to the altar. I knelt. I steadied the parchment in my hand. I put my right hand on the copy of the Constitutions. I tried to keep my voice clear and slow.

"I, Sister Mary Dolores Sodeman, in the presence of Almighty God, of the Blessed Virgin Mary, of all the saints, . . . make profession of the vows of Obedience, Chastity, and Poverty for three years, in accordance with the Rule of St. Augustine and the Constitutions of the Congregation of the Missionary Sisters of Our Lady of the Holy Rosary."

I kissed the silver crucifix the bishop held out to me. Mother Benedict fastened its chain behind my neck.

I kissed the black veil, as the bishop admonished me to

be dead to the world and alive with Christ to God. Mother Martin and Mother Benedict arranged it over my white veil. I went back to my place, the bride of Christ.

After divorcing me, Nancy wandered here and there about the country, remarried, divorced again, and finally joined a church—the renegade American Catholic Church. Her new congregation did not recognize the pope or his hierarchy. She called herself Nasira Alma.

Just before hepatitis C killed her in 1998, she wrote to me from Oregon. I wrote back and told her of my life since we separated, of my family and beautiful daughter, and of my sweet memories of our brief time together. She responded only days before dying with a final photo of herself in a T-shirt; LOVE was emblazoned across the front.

Nancy never forgot her passion for Jesus; I realize now that she divorced his church, not Him. She was always meeting Jesus in the garden.

Every Christmas we sing carols that attempt to describe an event beyond description—the birth of divinity in a child. That child is the essence of the simplicity and innocence the Shakers attempted to practice.

As every parent knows, there are no words to sum up adequately a new life. It's useless to try. When my daughter was born I was in awe of her; especially, for some reason, her minuscule fingernails. How could anything be so perfect, I marveled, holding her for the first time and grasping her tiny hand. Clearly, I was living in wonderland, far beyond anything I could imagine, logically or emotionally. In my arms was evidence of the God of Wonder and Love. And watching her grow up I have been constantly reacquainted with that God. Her birth, and her life, brought me back to the simple spirit of the church.

Christmas is about a holy child, and it is a holiday for children. Few adults can fully recall the ecstasy of their first Christmases, but carols help take us there.

Our season started with Pop's annual photograph of his family—my brother, sister, me, Mom, and Pop—for the annual Christmas card. He never missed a year with the cards. He had constructed a darkroom and photo workshop under the cellar stairs, where he developed and printed his shots. He was especially enamored of a new gadget that enabled him to snap himself with the rest of us via a remote control cable.

About the time that Pop took his annual photograph, we began to practice carols at school for the holiday pageant. Most of us, whatever our current religious faith, or lack of it, still remember those hymns. They are, for almost all children of all denominations, the very first songs we memorized.

As a sixth-grade trumpet player, I was selected to attempt the first verse of "O Holy Night," a song with exceedingly high notes at the climax of "O night divine."

O holy night! The stars are brightly shining.
It is the night of the dear Savior's birth.
Long lay the world in sin and darkness pining
'Til He appeared and the soul felt the worth.
A thrill of hope the weary world rejoices
For yonder breaks a new and glorious morn!
Fall on your knees, O hear the angel voices!
O night divine! O night when Christ was born!
O night divine! O night, O night divine!

I was certain I'd never hit those high notes and would disgrace myself in front of parents, teachers, and students. I tried every dodge to get out of the ordeal, including faking an earache. But Mom would have none of my excuses.

And so it came to pass that I memorized the notes and trumpeted alone that evening. With only a slight cracking of tone, I hit the peak of the hymn's passion with relative precision, and made it through my performance without running off the stage or throwing up.

I still consider "O Holy Night" one of the perfect carols—but for the first verse only. The following verses are rather clichéd and silly.

Early in December, Pop climbed the ladder to the attic and handed down the boxes that stored the Lionel train set—the tracks, the station, the cattle feed pen, the model village, an old-fashioned steam engine, freight cars, the transformer and switching gear, the diesel Santa Fe Flyer engine and passenger cars (a light lit up the inside of the cars and we could see the passengers silhouetted). On the living-room floor, we pieced together a rail line around the edges of the room, under the Christmas tree and sometimes even out to the dining room and back again.

And on that divine birthday morning of all mornings, Bob, Ruth, and I huddled at first light at the top of the stairs, waiting for Mom and Pop to join us in the rush down to the Christmas tree to discover what Santa had left us, and what marvelous gifts Pop had been secretly making in the basement, off-limits to us for months before. (One year it was a terrific wooden wagon, with rubber-treaded, handcrafted wooden wheels and "Bill & Bob" painted on the side.)

And so, pajamaed and taking turns, as instructed by Mom, we unloaded our Christmas stockings first and then ripped into the wrapped stuff from relatives, Mom, Pop, and Santa. (We noticed Santa had finished off the milk and cookies we left for him by the fireplace the night before.) Wrapping paper and ribbons flew about the room or were used to decorate our mutts of the moment, Trixie and Duke.

In one shameful Christmas season, when I was approaching my

noisome adolescence, Mom and Pop asked what I wanted that year, and I demanded boxing gloves. My pacific father was particularly appalled by the request. I was pulling a manly pose for him. To my sorrow, he went for it. On Christmas Day I fitted on the gloves— Bob also got a pair—and we belted each other a few times. Our manliness proven, the gloves went back in their boxes, never to reappear. They sit in some closet, somewhere, evidence of my final Christmas as a child.

Now the Christmas carols bring back those days. Somehow, they often turn even the most hardened among us into children again, if only briefly.

These hymns record improbable events—a virgin impregnated by a God, giving birth to a blameless son. We all know this is a retelling of numerous ancient myths, starting with Leda's affair with Zeus, cleverly disguised as a swan. But we don't care, so hungry are we for innocence. We sing of a star that wandered across the sky like a global positioning satellite, to lead pilgrims to the manger. A wandering star. Impossible. Yet we sing away our doubts and smother them in happiness.

And in our singing we hope that we can cause the universe to comply. The longing is from all of us—believers, sort-of-believers, agnostics, atheists, members of other faiths. If only our singing would make this story true. Innocence is born. A miracle in itself. He's here! Night of all nights. In all of cosmic time, none other like it. What hymn can capture all of this?

Isaac Watts's "Joy to the World" rockets to joy better than any other carol, I think:

> Joy to the world! The Lord is come!
> Let earth receive her King;
> Let every heart prepare Him room,
> And heav'n and nature sing.

And heav'n and nature sing.
And heaven, and heaven and nature sing.
Joy to the world! The Saviour reigns;
Let men their songs employ;
While fields and floods, rocks, hills and plains
Repeat the sounding joy,
Repeat the sounding joy
Repeat, repeat the sounding joy.

That first word—Joy. No messing around here. Right up front! This song is about that. And all of nature resounds with that elation. "Fields, floods, rocks, hills and plains repeat the sounding joy." Every atom of the physical world is dancing. And then Watts, throwing away caution, concludes with that soft, bedazzling finish— repeated over and over, as if the singer is hypnotized: "And wonders of His love, and wonders of His love, and wonders of His love, and wonders of His love."

Watts's lyrics were written about 1719, and this is one of six hundred hymns he wrote during his life. As I noted earlier, this father of English hymnody was one of the first to believe that hymns could be of modern composition and not just rephrasing of psalms, thus beginning a musical revolution in Reformed worship.

The music is by George Frederick Handel as arranged by the American Lowell Mason. We can thank both of them for this rousing song, almost a march tune that we can proclaim as we stride into the New Year. It's an aria of innocence we can sing all year, as long as our joy remains.

But unfortunately few Christmas hymns are sung beyond the season. So many of us refuse to rise to the occasion in spring, summer, or fall. All that happy musical chatter about harp-strumming angels, a virgin in labor, and the new heir to the line of David (which is obviously not so since God is the father and not Joseph) grows thin as soon as the eggnog wears off. And the explosive passions of love, brotherhood, and peace inspired by this Child's birth quiet down as the busy-lifestyle-year resumes.

Even rollicking carols like "We Three Kings of Orient Are," "The First Noel," "Hark the Herald Angels Sing," "It Came Upon a Midnight Clear," and "O Come All Ye Faithful" lose their bounce out of season and become unfashionable to sing out loud.

However, I think a few carols do survive the season. I can sing them after the Christmas tree tinsel has been packed away. They last because they are profound yet simple. "Away in a Manger" is such a carol.

> Away in a manger, no crib for His bed,
> The little Lord Jesus laid down His sweet head.
> The stars in the sky looked down where He lay,
> The little Lord Jesus asleep in the hay.
>
> The cattle are lowing, the Baby awakes,
> But little Lord Jesus, no crying He makes.
> I love thee Lord Jesus, look down from the sky,
> And stay by my cradle till morning is nigh.

"Away in a Manger" is a nursery-school song, first published in the Evangelical Lutheran Church's *Children's Book for Schools and Families* (Philadelphia, 1885). The tune "Cradle Song" was composed for these lyrics by William James Kirkpatrick, a compiler and editor of camp-meeting and gospel hymns. No singing of floods, rocks, and hills here. Just a boy baby asleep in the hay, the stars in place above him as they have been forever, the cattle lowing. Jesus wakes briefly, does not cry, and the hymn asks Him to stay by the singer's side until morning, and forever.

It's a child's plea for love and tenderness, but I'd suggest it as a song for almost anybody sleepless in the middle of the night. Even just the name Jesus said over and over, a mantra of eternal, unconditional love, will let you drift off. Nothing else matters except that love. And this cradle song is an improvement on the latest obsessively advertised sleeping pill concoction from the drug industry.

"O Little Town of Bethlehem," written by Phillips Brooks in 1868, with music by Lewis Henry Reiner, may not immediately seem to be a summertime-singable hymn. But it is a lovely poem that transforms Bethlehem into a place not unlike the village in Thornton Wilder's *Our Town*.

> O little town of Bethlehem,
> How still we see thee lie;
> Above thy deep and dreamless sleep
> The silent stars go by;
> Yet in thy dark streets shineth
> The everlasting Light.
> The hopes and fears of all the years
> Are met in thee tonight.
> For Christ is born of Mary,
> And gathered all above
> While mortals sleep, the angels keep
> Their watch of wondering love.
> O morning stars, together
> Proclaim the holy birth,
> And praises sing to God the King,
> And peace to men on earth!

Bethlehem is any town anywhere in the world. It's the middle of the night, quiet, dark. Everybody is asleep. The silent stars go on their way as always. But in one street a spiritual light shines. The hopes and fears of all time are found in this unsuspecting everyman's village.

Phillips Brooks, one of the most eloquent preachers of his time—"The Prince of the Pulpit," he was dubbed—traveled from his church, Holy Trinity (Episcopal) in Philadelphia, to Bethlehem and wrote the lyrics soon thereafter. Lewis Henry Reiner, organist, choir director, and Sunday School superintendent at Brooks's church, composed the music especially for the new hymn.

Brooks has discarded eloquence here. Rather than attempting to describe that night, he asks the singer to travel with him 1,868 years into the past. We are there. And the effect is tremendous—not unlike that of the hymn "Were You There?" We stand on the hill with Brooks and see that slumbering town beneath us. All of its citizens expect that the next day will be much like all the days before—indeed, eons of days before. But we watchers know that somewhere down there in the dark, the everlasting light has just begun to flicker. In any season of the year, the singer can climb that hill and see that village in his imagination.

In later verses we get none of the shouting angels. Here they keep a watch of "wondering love," a love so profound that even the angels can only wonder.

In the third verse, as in "Silent Night," the silence becomes almost palpable. "How silently" the gift is given as the town dreams. In this verse, the organ or piano usually drops out and we can hear our own voices, unaided, singing of the silence. And the transition to the final line of verse three is equally effective. No sudden conversions here. No born-again tears. We move into the present and all the towns of the world. "No ear may hear His coming . . . where meek souls will receive Him, still, the dear Christ enters in." A Shaker vision of the Second Coming.

And finally, joined again by the organ or piano, the final verse addresses Christ today, any day, not especially Christmas, and the singer asks Him to descend and "abide with us." No trumpets or earthquakes or Revelation pyrotechnics to announce Him. Just that lovely word "abide," as in the hymn "Abide With Me." This is a carol that transcends its season because of its everydayness, its lack of birthday fireworks.

Lyrics by literary masters might be presumed to outlast any Christmas season and reach for hymn immortality by making a more profound and thoughtful examination of religion. Surprisingly, this is almost never the case. Not only do poems written by literary sorts not make it into the ages; they seldom make it into the hymn books.

Robert Frost ("Oh Give Us Pleasure in the Flowers"), Langston Hughes ("Heaven Heaven Heaven Is the Place"), e. e. cummings ("Purer Than Purest Pure"), Mark Van Doren ("Praise Him Who Makes Us Happy"), Walt Whitman ("All the Past We Leave Behind"), Emily Dickinson ("If I Can Stop One Heart from Breaking"), Ralph Waldo Emerson ("We Love the Venerable House"), and G. K. Chesterton ("O God of Earth and Altar") all attempted sacred lyrics, but their words are infrequently sung. Perhaps intellectual musings are not what most worshippers want or need. Hymns are, after all, about worship—not literary distinction.

There are, however, at least three grand exceptions, and one of them is a Christmas carol.

Poet John Greenleaf Whittier's (1807–92) "Dear Lord and Father of Mankind," written in 1872, is still included in many hymnals, and while very much a hymn of the Victorian period, is lovely to sing still.

> O Sabbath rest by Galilee
> O calm of hills above,
> Where Jesus knelt to share with Thee
> The silence of eternity
> Interpreted by love!

"Jerusalem," by William Blake (1757–1827), poet, engraver, and painter, made the transition from literature to popular hymn.

Blake would have been amazed. While seldom sung in the United States, "Jerusalem" is as popular in England as "America the Beautiful" is here.

> And did those feet in ancient time
> Walk upon England's mountains green?
> And was the Holy Lamb of God
> On England's pleasant pastures seen?
> And did the countenance divine
> Shine forth upon our clouded hills?
> And was Jerusalem builded here
> Among these dark satanic mills?
>
> Bring me my bow of burning gold!
> Bring me my arrows of desire!
> Bring me my spear! O clouds, unfold!
> Bring me my chariot of fire!
> I will not cease from mental fight,
> Nor shall my sword sleep in my hand,
> Till we have built Jerusalem
> In England's green and pleasant land.

What amazes me about the English fondness for this hymn is that it is more of an insult to industrial Britain than a compliment. The poet wonders if Jesus walked there in ancient times: "Was the Holy Lamb of God/On England's pleasant pastures seen?" And was Jerusalem built among "these dark satanic mills"? (Imagine an American singing that line about the factories of Detroit.) Blake longs for the day when such mills are destroyed and "we have built Jerusalem/In England's green and pleasant land."

England's prime minister, Tony Blair, declared that this is his favorite hymn "because it is symbolic of my feelings for New Labour." Some might say that Blake's poem has been hijacked, but however perceived, it endures.

The one Christmas carol by a literary light that is still with us is Christina Rossetti's (1830–94) "In the Bleak Midwinter," a poem written about 1872 and not set to music until over a decade after her death. We would not know the poem as a hymn had it not been adapted by Gustav Theodore Holst (1874–1934)—known today for his symphony *The Planets*. It was published in *The English Hymnal* in 1906.

This carol is especially close to me because I had never heard of it until my daughter sang it as a duet during her school's Christmas concert. Like me with my trumpet, attempting the high notes in "O Holy Night," Holly was nervous before her performance.

In the little Westover School chapel, before students and parents, as a piano accompanied them, Holly and her friend, Victoria, held hands and sang beautifully. It was a night very much like that described in Rossetti's poem—bleak, quite cold, "Earth hard as iron, water like a stone."

The service was traditional and followed biblical accounts, as read by students. Eve took most of the blame for man's fall—a startling message for a girl's school, I thought. After Eve's mistake with the serpent and the fruit sampling that followed, we needed a messiah to free us from sin. Isaiah predicted that He was on his way, and was quoted at length. Other students read about Mary's virginity and the Annunciation.

But Rossetti's hymn takes us back to that night so that we experience it immediately. Like Phillips Brooks, she imagines the land itself, a real place. The entire first verse impresses us not with God's glory, but with how frozen and miserable the earth was—as were, perhaps, the minds of the people of that long ago town.

Who knew they needed a child to proclaim love to them? They slept their dreamless, Bethlehem sleep, not suspecting how unfrozen the world would soon become.

"Snow had fallen, snow on snow/Snow on snow," Rossetti repeats. The winter seemed endless. "Bleak," she says twice. "Bleak." This is a poem and a hymn we feel in our bones.

IN THE
BLEAK MIDWINTER

CRANHAM   Irregular

Christina Rossetti, c. 1872; alt.

Gustav Theodore Holst, 1906

1. In the bleak mid - win - ter, Frost-y wind made moan,
2. Our God, heaven can - not hold Him, Nor earth sus - tain;
3. An - gels and arch - an - gels May have gath-ered there,
4. What can I give Him, Poor as I am?

Earth stood hard as i - ron, Wa - ter like a stone;
Heaven and earth shall flee a-way When He comes to reign:
Cher - u - bim and ser - a-phim Thronged the air;
If I were a shep - herd, I would bring a lamb;

Snow had fall - en, snow on snow, Snow on snow,
In the bleak mid - win - ter A sta - ble-place suf - ficed
But His moth - er on - ly, In her maid - en bliss,
If I were a wise man, I would do my part;

In the bleak mid - win - ter, Long a - go.
The Lord God in - car - nate, Je - sus Christ.
Wor-shiped the be - lov - ed With a kiss.
Yet what I can I give Him: Give my heart.

But this frosty immobility is nothing to the God of love. "Heaven cannot hold Him," let alone a little ice. And he's uninterested in fancy lodgings. A stable was OK. No need to seem impressive by human standards.

Rossetti doesn't rely on the stock worship glories of some other carols. "Angels and archangels may have gathered there." May? She doesn't really care if this was true. All that angel stuff isn't really major. Same for cherubim and seraphim. Here's what is:

> But His mother only
> In her maiden bliss,
> Worshiped the beloved
> With a kiss.

This mother's kiss is at the center of the poem and lifts us far above all the hyperbole of other carols. Even if you believe none of this story, the simple kiss, any mother's kiss, is about as rock-bottom true as it ever gets.

In the final verse, Rossetti, again like Brooks, returns us to the present. The poet asks what can she give the child that would in any way be comparable to Mary's kiss? A shepherd brings a lamb, a wise man does his "part" (a rather skeptical idea of what a wise man is able to donate—he'll do whatever he can, which may not be much).

What is the greatest gift for the baby? "What can I give Him: Give my heart." In other words, her whole being. No other gift means as much. "Simple Gifts," "He Lives!" "In the Garden" all say the same.

Rossetti's quiet, lovely poem about a holy child's birth was sung to me by my sixteen-year-old child, who in her birth and childhood taught me again and again what really matters. And it's all so simple.

At the concert's end, the 186 girls of the school proceeded past their parents two by two, as we held lighted candles. My candle refused to stay lit and Holly smiled at my predicament as she walked by. Was God trying to tell me something with this candle? If so, exactly what, I wondered—ever alert for messages from the Thin Places.

Out of the chapel and down the school's hall they walked, singing a chant until they were far in the depths of the school, their voices fading away. That diminishing chant was incredibly moving. Every parent in the room longed to keep them in that moment, in their pure singing, in their youth, even as Rossetti captured an ancient night of innocence and never let it go.

III

Amazing Grace

SONGS OF WONDER

AMAZING GRACE

For by grace are ye saved through faith . . . — Ephesians 2:8

AMAZING GRACE
American Melody
Carrell and Clayton's *Virginia Harmony*
Harmonized by Edwin O. Excell

John Newton
John P. Rees, stanza 5

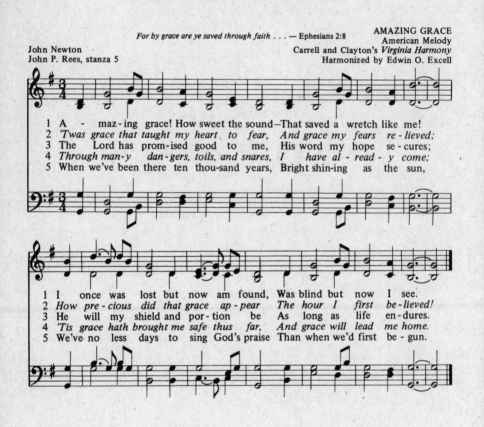

1 A - maz-ing grace! How sweet the sound—That saved a wretch like me!
2 *'Twas grace that taught my heart to fear,* *And grace my fears re-lieved;*
3 The Lord has prom-ised good to me, His word my hope se-cures;
4 *Through man-y dan-gers, toils, and snares,* *I have al-read-y come;*
5 When we've been there ten thou-sand years, Bright shin-ing as the sun,

1 I once was lost but now am found, Was blind but now I see.
2 *How pre-cious did that grace ap-pear* *The hour I first be-lieved!*
3 He will my shield and por-tion be As long as life en-dures.
4 *'Tis grace hath brought me safe thus far,* *And grace will lead me home.*
5 We've no less days to sing God's praise Than when we'd first be-gun.

As I said about "Simple Gifts," some hymns have meant so much to me and to so many singers over the centuries that I hesitate to write mere words about them. "Amazing Grace" is such a hymn.

From the stone edifices of the wealthy to the wooden worship boxes of the poor, to people of all ages, races, and nations, this hymn about the wonder of grace has inspired and encouraged.

As one woman in Bill Moyers's vivid film documentary *Amazing Grace* puts it: "Whenever the people start to sing this hymn tears start coming out of my eyes. I don't understand it. It's like roots reaching 'way down deep."

Judy Collins remembers singing "Amazing Grace" with Fannie Lou Hamer at a 1964 voter registration drive in Mississippi when the danger to them was very real. She recalls that even the police were moved by the hymn. Later, in concert, she says the hymn gave her and her audience "a sense of other dimensions . . . a mystical experience that is indescribable."

Johnny Cash says: "This is a song with no guile. Those lyrics are straight ahead, honest, gut-level and heart-level. . . . There are some songs that make a difference and that song makes a difference."

And opera diva Jessye Norman wonders, "Is it the text or the tune? Whatever. . . . This song is profoundly moving."

One of the miracles of this hymn is that tune. Nobody knows where it came from. The music now permanently linked to "Amazing Grace" is called "New Britain," suggesting an English origin. One hymnal calls this "an American melody." Another guesses it is Scottish, from the Scots settlers of Kentucky. And Jessye Norman suggests it might have originated with African slaves and was ironically joined with the words of Newton, a former captain in the slave trade.

Like "Slane," the ancient tune of "Be Thou My Vision," little more is known about "New Britain."

What is known is that many words have been grafted on to the original stanzas of "Amazing Grace," so welcoming is the music. While I consider only Newton's original words here, several hymnals list verses of uncertain origin that have been tacked on. Newton's words are the constant heart, particularly the first three stanzas that survive in most versions.

Curiously, he did not include the name of Jesus in "Amazing Grace," although many of the hymns he wrote were standard renderings of the theme of the crucifixion and sacrifice of God's only son.

Because this is not an orthodox Jesus hymn, it can be sung by any congregation in praise of God's love, whatever denomination or religion. In short, it is a world hymn.

Astonishingly, the lyrics open with a word construed as almost meaningless today—"amazing." This has become advertising hype . . . the amazing new can opener, new car, new computer, right up there with "awesome," cheapened by the media. If we were to write a new hymn today with such a term, it would be laughable.

But this *is* a hymn of amazement, in all the original sense of the word, and no secular cant will dim what Newton does next with a very few, very ordinary words.

The second word, "grace," is a term so profound that perhaps only music can attempt to define it. Bill Moyers calls grace "the transforming power that can change a life." The dictionary tries: "a state of mind pleasing to God, the power from God that enables one to achieve such a state." I try to describe "grace" as evidence of the wonder of God's love known to your very source, to your deepest heart and soul.

For John Newton, grace is given to you by God. You can't seek grace, never deserve it. Nineteenth-century evangelist Dwight Moody had a different idea: Grace is available to those who repent and seek God. If you make an honest effort, you will receive grace.

In the late twentieth century grace was often described as a sudden insight or a cosmic force. Theologian Paul Tillich described grace as a wave of light that suddenly breaks through despair: "It is as though a voice were saying, 'You are accepted, accepted by that which is greater than you, and the name of which you do not know.'" For nonbelievers grace might be described as a sudden insight through meditation.

Whatever grace is to Newton, to Moody, to Tillich, to New Age gurus, it is always full of wonder, and beyond our rational understanding.

Newton describes grace as both a word and a sound. "How sweet the sound." (In his original version, this phrase was in parentheses.) He *hears* the sweetness of grace. And in the next stanza grace appears to him: "How precious did that grace appear." Newton savors grace by sound and sight and makes it sensual to us.

Grace "saved" Newton from drowning in a storm at sea, from spiritual blindness, from self-loathing, from myriad "dangers, toils, and snares."

He describes himself as a "wretch." How marvelous is that word "wretch." I love to hit it hard and loud when singing. Like grace, it is the sound that counts. "Wretch" says it all, mightily— vile, contemptible. In my drinking days, it was a word I recognized in morning-after hangovers. Nobody needs a dictionary definition for wretch. We have all been there in some way at some time in the past. In fact, the word is so strong, so disturbing that once it was removed by some churches from the hymn—too coarse for nice Sunday ears.

The next line softens "wretch"—"I once was lost but now am found." Being lost is the stuff of nightmares. In mine, I wake up in a strange city, usually in ratty clothes and often with no shoes, no money, no idea how to get home, or even what home might be, begging strangers for advice, being scorned, ignored.

Everybody has a version of this dream. We have all been lost for a moment as children and will never forget it. To be lost, as an adult, is just as bad if not worse. To lose your idea of who you are, where you are, why you are doing what you are doing—that's lost. And Newton, once the perpetual scoundrel lost in life, and at sea, knew well the impact of this terrifying term.

But immediately after "lost," Newton snaps us up with another simple, tremendous word—"found." The parent finds the child, the wife and husband reconcile, friends rediscover friends, culture is led back to its roots, the dreamer wakes up from a nightmare.

But being found is not what the singer does on his or her own. The line is "am found." It is not "I got myself found" or "I attained self-esteem" (ghastly term). Being found, in this hymn, is done for you from a source other than yourself.

In the Alcoholics Anonymous *Big Book,* the drunk can only be helped when he decides to "let go and let God." Grace finds us, and is always there waiting to do just that.

And finally, in one of the most moving endings to any stanza in any hymn, Newton uses the word "blind"—another nightmare vision. Those of us who can indeed see imagine that we are not blind, and we pray that we never will be. We think that we can see, but of course we notice only a few things. Most of life is microscopic or even out of sight to the most powerful microscope, known by its effect on surrounding particles or merely through theory. We can't see certain wavelengths. We imagine we can see precisely what we need to see, but in truth we are almost as sight-less as blind worms in a cave.

Suddenly Newton announces "but now I see." I can seldom sing that word "see" without a big gulp. Such a simple word and it simply soars. We can see, and only grace allows that sight.

My good secular friends don't understand this seeing business. What vision precisely is it that I see? It seems all I am doing is recall-ing my childhood—obvious nostalgia for what is gone forever. Per-haps the wine is influencing him again, they think.

And afterward, like any person with faith, I often wonder in dark periods what it is that I see. Why is that word in "Amazing Grace" so strong? Why does it mean more at this place in this hymn than it seems any word should?

The answer is that "see" describes exactly what happens in a re-ligious epiphany, such as my own awakening on the Ellsworth Road in Maine (recalled later), when I thought my daughter was dying and I vowed to follow her. Love flooded the landscape and my mind. It was palpable. The earth caught fire. Call it the flame of the Holy Ghost, call it what you wish. But that is what "see" means to me.

And suddenly it is all plain: We are not just a few dollars worth of chemicals in a water solution, a bladder of hungers and pains soon to be pissed away. We are surrounded by and we contain some-thing huge: a spirit and a power that I call love. It's overwhelming when we know that love plainly. The wretched worm in the cave senses what is beyond. The worm sees.

For me, and for Newton, a vision is often followed by a period of blindness. We forget. The world is constantly too much with us. Stuff to do, fusses and worries, passing glories. We are far from God. I have been there often, as was Newton, even after his conver-sion. Countless singers know Newton's experience. That's why this hymn is so personal for them. Newton's memoir is their own confession, a testimony—a stand-up-in-church witness to the wonder of God. There's not a false word here. It is a cry from the heart without compromise or theology or apology.

In verse two, we encounter the word "fear"—"'Twas grace that taught my heart to fear." This is a shocking idea in modern times. What's to fear? There's a drug for every anxiety. We are a very comfortable people—with only vague churnings about terrorism or stray asteroids interjected like annoying bugs. Religious fear has become archaic, mere superstition.

Newton never says exactly what this fear is. I suspect it is the fear of being removed from grace, doomed to a present and perhaps future hell without the divine light. Again, a wretch.

Our modern tragedy is that we don't want to know what he's talking about. Our spirit is numb. But grace remains, whether we want to see it or not.

In the third verse, Newton writes of the "dangers, toils, and snares" that grace has brought him through. In his diaries he described them: "How industriously is Satan served. A common drunkard and profligate is but a petty sinner to what I was. I had the ambition of a Caesar, of an Alexander. I wanted to rank in wickedness among the foremost of the human race."

In Bill Moyers's documentary, Johnny Cash sings to audiences of prisoners who have known plenty of dangers, toils, and snares. "For that three minutes the song is going on, everybody is free . . . I could be in a dungeon, but when I sing that song, I am free as a breeze," Cash says. A prisoner adds, "The only way out is up," and "Amazing Grace" takes him there.

Jessye Norman tells Moyers that verse three is her favorite. "There's such a wonderful calm I feel when I sing it—an uncomplicated feeling as one felt as a child. There's such hope at the end. I've gotten this far because of grace and the same thing that has brought me this far will carry me the rest of the way."

Perhaps the most stunning argument for grace is the history of this hymn. Its journey has been like the mystery of grace itself.

The story of John Newton and the creation of "Amazing Grace" is usually completely skewed. The popular version is that Newton, captain of slave ships, almost perished in a storm at sea. Because he was spared he converted to Christianity, freed his slave cargo, and launched a crusade against the slave trade.

It didn't happen like that.

Steve Turner's definitive history of this hymn, *Amazing Grace* (Ecco, 2002) to which I am deeply indebted for insight and information, outlines a chronology of Newton's life that is disturbing to those who wish it went the other way. Like St. Paul, Newton's conversion was indeed swift, but the meaning of it was a long time coming for him. He saw through a glass darkly but decades passed before he was face to face with his faith. Because this hymn is a synopsis of his life, I will consider that life in some detail.

John Newton was born on July 24, 1725, in Wapping, a hub of ocean commerce in London. His father, a merchant captain also named John Newton, was remembered by his son as aloof, and often away at sea for years on end. "I always feared him," said Newton.

He was raised by his mother, Elizabeth, a devout Christian who attended nonconformist religious services near their home. Hoping that he would become a minister, she drilled him in his catechism. She was as warm and loving as his father was cold and strict. When Newton was seven, she was infected with tuberculosis and soon died.

Newton was shipped off to a boarding school where his spirit was crushed by a harsh schoolmaster. The boy suffered a breakdown, his memory failed, and his hunger for books was extinguished.

When Newton was eleven, his father took him off to sea with him. For almost two decades, ships and their commerce, eventually slaves, became his life.

For many of those earlier years he struggled to retain the Christianity learned from his mother. He kept a spiritual journal, read the Bible daily, fasted, and became a vegetarian. The result of all this rigor, he reported, was that he found no joy or peace but became "gloomy and stupid."

His spiritual devotion was often replaced with undisciplined excess and religious indifference. He indulged freely in vices that, in the decorous tradition of the time, he did not detail, but we may assume included sex and drunkenness, plus his confessed foul language and blasphemy. Newton wrote that he was "a superb orator for the Antichrist."

The one check on his decline was young Mary Catlett, the daughter of family friends. He later wrote to her from sea, "The first day I saw you I began to love you. The thoughts of one day meriting you (and I believe nothing less could have done it) roused me from a dull insensible melancholy."

From then on, if his religion had died, his love for his vision of Mary never did. During the messy chronology of his seafaring youth, he was almost always working his way back to her from some port or beach or jungle.

Barely a year after declaring his love for young Mary, he was press-ganged into the crew of HMS *Harwich,* a 976-ton warship with a crew of 350 sailors, about to sail with a huge fleet to protect English merchant ships. War with France was imminent.

Press-ganging was not a pleasant procedure. The navy, often shorthanded, recruited thugs to haunt dockside pubs and capture men too drunk to resist. They would wake up onboard, enlisted against their will. Winston Churchill once remarked that the English navy was built on the pillars of "rum, sodomy, and flogging."

As to Newton, we have no hint of sodomy as a personal indulgence, but it surrounded him. He was not a stranger to rum and insubordination plus episodes of going AWOL (once to see Mary before shipping out), for which he was flogged in front of the *Harwich* crew.

In April 1745 the *Harwich* sailed for Africa and India—a five-year trip. Desperate to return to his Mary, Newton got himself transferred to a merchant ship that was headed for Sierra Leone to pick up slaves.

Still the arrogant fornicator (the rape of slave girls was common), he did not endear himself to the new captain either. Within six months he was dismissed and went to work for a slave trader on an island off the African coast.

His employer was an unnamed Englishman, with an African mistress named P.I., the daughter of a local chief of some stature. She herself had many slaves to tend to her needs. For some reason, never explained by Newton, she disliked him intensely. When her master/lover was away in the interior searching for prime specimens, Newton came down with malaria; convulsions, vomiting, diarrhea, and hallucinations. He slept in the dirt in his only clothes, with a log for a pillow. He probably would have died from starvation if not for the kindness of slaves who brought him morsels of their food.

Broken in body, but not yet humbled in heart, Newton was desperate to escape this infernal island. He scribbled letters to Mary and to his father, begging for rescue. He handed the letters to departing slaves with little hope that they would reach England.

But then his fortunes (or God's favor, as he would later describe it) changed. He was employed by another trader and traveled up rivers to inland villages where local chiefs were happy to exchange captives for English guns and pots and pans. The slave trade was their ticket to regional power. Newton was feasted and honored and offered sexual delights.

He was comfortable with the natives. He admired their customs, their usually peaceful ways, and their lack of religious requirements: They worshipped a sort of god but without rules. In order to scare off evil they invoked the shades of ancestors. For a bountiful harvest, they donated wine and food to the new moon.

With Christianity dead in mind and soul, and thoughts of Mary becoming distant, young Newton was close to his heart of darkness. As G. K. Chesterton put it later: "When a man ceases to believe in God, he doesn't believe in nothing. He believes in anything."

But by chance or God's grace a passing ship, the *Greyhound,* whose captain had been instructed by Newton's father to look for his son—he had miraculously received Newton's letter—arrived to trade for slaves. Newton had to be persuaded to leave. Only thoughts of seeing Mary again convinced him to sail away on the *Greyhound.*

On March 9, 1748, Newton's life—and the world's hymn book— changed. Somewhere off the coast of Newfoundland an immense storm struck the *Greyhound* and was ripping it apart. Like all slavers, it was poorly built, not expected to last long. And the human cargo wasn't precious, certainly less so than a cargo of bullion or beeswax.

At one point, John Newton cried out, "The Lord have mercy on us!" He was shocked by his words. Where had they come from?

Somehow the ship made it to Ireland. Soon after they arrived, another storm, which would have sunk them at sea, swept in from the Atlantic.

Stunned by his outcry and the sequence of events, Newton visited a church where he fell on his knees, took the sacraments, and surrendered to the faith of his childhood—even though not yet comprehending what was happening to him or what he really thought.

This then is the grace he wrote about years later; the grace that fell on him directly that indeed had been hounding him and pro- tecting him for years.

John Newton, the wretch, had been saved, physically and spiri- tually. But he was spiritually a child, remembering only what his mother had taught him. His pilgrimage had just started.

As soon as he returned to England, he shyly asked Mary to marry him. She did not discourage him. After one more trip to sea—as a first mate aboard the slaver *Brownlow* (221 slaves transported, sixty dead en route)—he made Mary his wife on February 1, 1750. With that voyage he had proved to himself that he was a worthy seaman, able to take orders, and he proved to her that he was a bountiful provider.

He was twenty-five. His career as a slave-ship captain was yet to begin. At this point in his life, it is easy to scoff at Newton and his new faith. His pursuit of a vocation in the slave trade is morally unsettling. Any critic could question the worth of a Christian calling if it allowed a young man to continue in such evil.

But as a constant backslider, I can appreciate to a slight degree his lack of consistency. One knows what one should do, but very seldom does it. In college, as a depressed sophomore with vague thoughts of suicide, I had hit bottom. All my attempts to discover The Truth had failed. There seemed to be nothing real, or worth a continuing quest. I was rescued by an idea that appeared in my own spiritual storm, an epiphany: "Life is sacred." This is where you start, my epiphany indicated. I am sacred, you are sacred, all living beings are sacred. You can set out on your knowledge quest from no other point, otherwise why bother to begin at all? My philosophical maxim, tacked over my desk, carried me for two decades, until I rejoined the church. But I seldom consulted it, occupying myself instead with drinking, sexual antics, and literary busyness.

That Newton was found and then lost, by his own admission, to periods of vice—and to moral blindness about slavery—doesn't surprise me. To see a vision—to really see and to keep on seeing every day—was a tough task in a harsh and practical world that, then as now, denied spiritual visions at every turn. For Newton, there was money to be made in slavery, a career to be constructed, a woman to please.

He made three voyages as a captain between 1750 and 1754. During this time he kept meticulous diaries, still valued today as records of the slave trade, and he wrote constantly to Mary.

He first captained the *Duke of Argyle,* sailing from England in late 1750 to trade up and down the African coast, collecting 174 slaves and delivering them to Charleston, South Carolina, returning in May 1751. Twenty-eight slaves died en route, plus seven crewmen.

Newton's next two voyages were on *The African,* which set out in June 1752 and again in October 1753, on both occasions hauling slaves from East Africa to the Caribbean.

Newton was responsible for inspecting slaves before boarding. He accepted only children, able young men, and women who could have children. Over half the offerings were rejected as too old, or otherwise unsuitable. In his diaries he notes that he spurned women for being "fallen breasted."

Steve Turner describes the slave deck in the hold: "Here, shackled in twos, the slaves were forced to lie side by side. It was cramped, dark and stifling. There was a continual noise of cries, screams, and different regional languages. Vomit, urine and feces combined to create a smell so pungent that the sailors could barely force themselves to go down."

On the deck above, Newton, according to Turner, kept a civilized veneer. He started each day with an hour of prayer in his chambers where he also taught himself French, read poetry, and studied mathematics. Often he corresponded with a minister back in England, attempting to understand the nuances of Calvinism. For his crew, he composed prayers.

On Sundays, all hands were ordered to attend full church services, complete with hymns and liturgy. Somehow they ignored the screams and stench wafting up from below them.

Did not Newton recall Jesus' great commandment to love God and thy neighbor as thyself? Perhaps he didn't conceive of these Africans as covered by the term "neighbor." Perhaps we can understand it like that, if indeed we can conceive of this horror at all.

In his diaries and letters to Mary, Newton expressed no remorse. By justification he offered the lame excuse that Africans had no words in their language for liberty, religion, and love, and thus were inferior. To Mary he wrote, off the coast of Sierra Leone, "How greatly God has distinguished me!"

Forty years later, Newton reported that all along he had "felt the disagreeableness of the business very strongly . . . but I considered it as the line of life which God in His providence, had allotted me and as a cross which I ought to bear." After all, I note even St. Paul obliquely approved of slavery, suggesting only that masters recognize their slaves as brothers and sisters.

The young captain lived in a society that overwhelmingly approved of the slave trade. Blacks were lost to the glories of European culture. Left in Africa they would all have ended in hell. Slavery was their ticket to salvation. Newton and others thought of their business, if they thought in such terms at all, as a favor for the slaves. And then, too, there was all that money. The potentates of the trade, like mill owners who abused children, were able to afford prominent pews in the Church of England.

At the end of 1754, Newton was about to depart on another slave expedition when grace intruded once again. The young captain was suddenly struck down in a fit of "apoplexy." His doctor ordered him never to sail again. God's grace, as he later interpreted it, had saved him for another calling. He had much more to see.

Newton's life changed rapidly after his mysterious collapse. He attended a variety of evangelical services in the Liverpool area and was invited to testify about his miraculous conversion. Eventually he felt a call to the ministry in the Church of England, which he favored because of its Calvinistic insistence on the power of grace.

A Baptist minister asked Newton to write the story of his sea change. This manuscript was read by Lord Dartmouth, a wealthy and powerful evangelical who owned much of the land around the village of Olney. In short order, he had not only persuaded the presiding bishop to ordain Newton at Olney, but paid for the publication of Newton's autobiography, which became a huge commercial success.

Suddenly, the former fornicator, drunk, and blasphemer was propelled to the forefront of the British evangelical movement, a friend to the wealthy and powerful.

Through his passionate conviction and his connection to the

common people, Newton became a popular priest. The Olney congregation grew so fast that after-church gatherings were required for hymns and prayers (admission by ticket only). Newton created special meetings for the children—a model for the modern Sunday School—and visited people at work, attended to the needs of the poor and, as he was now a national figure, preached on national issues, but never spoke of slavery.

Every Sunday, with the influence of his close friend, the poet William Cowper, Newton composed hymns to accompany his sermons. Few of these hymns are sung today, which makes the survival and the immense popularity of "Amazing Grace" all the more amazing.

Newton created his hymns for the people of Olney; the laborers, carpenters, lace-makers, and others, many of them illiterate. He insisted that his hymns be not poems but verses "for the use of plain people."

He avoided sharp statements of creed that might divide denominations. In person and in his compositions he was a healer and a peacemaker. He wrote in his preface to *Olney Hymns,* "I hope most of these hymns, being the fruit and expression of my own experience, will coincide with the views of real Christians of all denominations . . . I am not conscious of having written a single line with an intention to flatter or offend any person or party on earth."

"Amazing Grace" was composed in late December 1772, in a small attic room of the vicarage.

It was written to accompany a sermon based on Chronicles 17:16–17, in which God promised King David that he will make his name like "the names of the greatest men on earth," and David responded with wonder at God's goodness to him.

The words of "Amazing Grace" emphasize King David's sentiments, and certainly reflect Newton's life. If an autobiography can be contained in a few verses, this is the example. As Joan Baez remarked, almost two hundred years later, this was "the song of his life."

Here is the entire text, as Newton wrote it down. Note that "how sweet the sound" is almost a sigh.

Amazing grace! (how sweet the sound)
That saved a wretch like me!
I once was lost, but now am found
Was blind, but now I see.

'Twas grace that taught my heart to fear,
And grace my fears relieved:
How precious did that grace appear,
The hour I first believed!

Through many dangers, toils, and snares,
I have already come;
'Tis grace has brought me safe thus far,
And grace will lead me home.

The Lord has promised good to me.
His word my hope secures:
He will my shield and portion be,
As long as life endures.

Yes, when this flesh and heart shall fail,
And mortal life shall cease;
I shall possess within the vail,
A life of joy and peace.

The earth shall soon dissolve like snow,
The sun forbear to shine:
But God, who called me here below,
Will be forever mine.

"Amazing Grace" was probably recited without music at the church service that late December, or perhaps on New Year's Day 1773. It may have been sung to a familiar psalm tune in the gathering after church, but in any case, because of Calvin's dictates, no instruments accompanied its premiere.

The events of that day were not recorded in Newton's diary (now lost). That the hymn itself was not lost is due to the serendipitous publication of *Olney Hymns* in February 1779—the printing of one thousand copies underwritten by John Thornton, a wealthy Christian and director of the Bank of England. "Amazing Grace" is Hymn Number 41 in "On select texts of scripture" and it uses a portion of two pages.

All profits from the book were donated to Olney's poor. Soon after its publication, Newton was invited to a much larger parish in London—St. Mary Woolnoth, near the Bank of England, where he would spend the rest of his days and greatly expand his influence. Much later he would finally begin to speak out about slavery, as society around him, seemingly immune to the moral implications of the trade, began to be repulsed by it. Why it took him so long to denounce his former occupation is still unclear. Certainly he advertised his shame while recounting his conversion. But as yet slavery was not part of that shame.

Finally, in 1787, Newton published a ten-thousand-word essay, "Thoughts Upon The Africa Slave Trade," in which he stated that he was "bound in conscience to take shame on myself by a public confession which, however sincere, comes too late to prevent or repair the misery and mischief to which I have formerly been accessory." After years of suppressing his misgivings he declared the trade to be "cruel . . . oppressive . . . destructive . . . disgraceful . . . and unlawful." The harm done to the sailor was just as egregious as that inflicted on the slaves, said Newton. He recalled the rape of slave girls, the torture of disobedient slaves, and wanton murder. Slavery was destructive, not because of any biblical, legal, or social stigma attached to it, but simply because it "robbed the heart of every gentle and humane disposition."

John Newton, barely able to hear, speak, or read, died on December 21, 1807—the same year that Parliament banned the slave trade. He had continued preaching as long as possible about the grace that God had demonstrated to him during that storm—the day he began to "see."

John Newton became a healer and lover of all people, who cared little for doctrinal niceties. The direct, unadorned words of his hymn are a profound communication from one soul to millions. That it and his vision of grace have reached us is a testimony to the grace it celebrates, and also to the influence of the slaves he transported, and their descendants.

"Amazing Grace" has been little appreciated in England. As late as 1950, the hymn wasn't mentioned in an exhaustive biography of Newton published there.

As Turner emphasizes and details, it was in the United States that it was discovered and treasured by slaves, who altered it and added verses; and also by white pioneers who responded from their own experience to the struggle the hymn describes, plus the promise that grace would eventually lead them home.

"Amazing Grace" was often sung, to different tunes, at the Great Awakening gatherings of the early nineteenth century and was propelled to national notice in two books: *Southern Harmony* (1835), where it was joined to its present tune, "New Britain," for the first time; and *The Sacred Harp* (1844), the bible of shape note singing. Because of both books, "Amazing Grace" became an icon of southern religion. Through the worldwide ministry of preacher Dwight L. Moody and his song leader, Ira D. Sankey, who revolutionized evangelism and included the hymn in Sankey's phenomenally popular *Songs and Solos* (1875), it eventually reached the white community of churches.

It might have stayed there, as a song restricted to white churches, had it not been for the black community. The verse:

> When we've been there ten thousand years,
> Bright shining as the sun,
> We've no less days to sing God's praise
> Than when we first begun.

was tacked on to Newton's original by a white Chicago publisher and composer who may have lifted it from a stanza in Harriet Beecher Stowe's *Uncle Tom's Cabin* (1852); Stowe, in turn, took it from black tradition.

By the time of emancipation, an estimated fourteen thousand slaves were direct descendants of souls Newton had helped transport to Charleston, South Carolina, and forty thousand traced their ancestry to his Caribbean trips.

Slaves knew that Newton had been in a spiritual pit like their own. "Amazing Grace" was, after all, written by a man who described himself as "a servant of slaves in Africa," the lowest of the low. That he had been through "many dangers, toils, and snares" described the slaves' condition precisely, as did Newton's faith that grace would lead to a better place. "Amazing Grace" became a testimony of black survival and hope for liberation.

Slaves learned hymns in the churches of their white masters. Since they were kept illiterate, they had to memorize hymns they appreciated. If a hymn wasn't good enough to memorize, it was deemed not good enough to sing.

Because they were denied text or tune books, slaves held no fidelity to words or sound. They were blessedly free to improvise and therefore scrambled lyrics and music, often adding shouts, moans, repetitions, and interjections of their personal experiences. Preachers "lined out" the words of a song two lines at a time before singing and added two more lines after these were sung and so forth. The rest of the service became a free form of prayers and testimony and snatches of hymns, frequently lines from "Amazing Grace."

Because segregation kept black and white services apart, "Amazing Grace" followed its own trajectory in African-American churches. The first recordings of the hymn were made in 1926 by producers hungry to tap into "the race market." One featured the prominent "shouting preacher" Reverend J. M. Gates.

To Reverend Gates, "Amazing Grace" was a revered hymn from the old days, a tribute to the strong faith of his ancestors. "We're living in a scientific age now where people are trying to lay aside the old hymns and keep up with style. We're living in a time where Atlanta gets her style from New York and New York gets her style from Paris and Paris is getting her style from hell. Except we sing more of these old familiar hymns, we'll find ourselves in the same city," he proclaimed.

Because of its history in the black community, "Amazing Grace" would change into the blues-and-jazz-inspired free-form gospel music of the 1940s and 1950s, most evident in the 1947 epic recording of Mahalia Jackson for Apollo Records. Jackson lavished thirteen seconds on the first word of the hymn and two minutes on the first stanza, savoring every word and tone.

From her recordings and those of many other black gospel artists—James Cleveland, the Dixie Hummingbirds, Albertina Walker, the Mighty Clouds of Joy, the Blind Boys of Alabama, to name but a few—"Amazing Grace" was introduced to audiences who appreciated it as pure song and not merely religious music.

It was no surprise that the folk music movement of the 1920s through the 1960s appreciated the hymn. The first recording for "the hillbilly market" was made by Columbia Records in 1926 and featured the Wisdom Singers, a female vocal trio performing a cappella.

The father-and-son team of John and Alan Lomax was crucial in its own way. In 1932, hauling a 350-pound battery-powered recording device, the two crossed the South in the family Ford. Their goal was to save authentic grassroots music from the incursion of modern records, radio, and film. They logged sixteen thousand miles, recording local singers, and published the results in their book, *American Ballads and Folk Songs.*

The Lomaxes discovered Aunt Molly Jackson, a fifty-five-year-old white labor activist from the Kentucky mountains, who sang "Amazing Grace" in her own style for their recording device. Later, they recorded eleven more variations.

The Lomax influence on the university-educated audiences was profound. Here they found the real voice of black and white working people, plus inspiration to create their own folk tunes. Singers Pete Seeger and Woody Guthrie crossed the country performing folk ballads at workers' and political action rallies, and, in the 1940s, Seeger's group The Weavers used "Amazing Grace" frequently. For Seeger, an agnostic and committed communist, his appreciation of the hymn seemed a contradiction, but he explained about Newton, "I say that if he could turn his life around like that it gives us all hope that we can turn this world around."

Seeger's adaptation of "Amazing Grace" as a secular pop song persuaded others, like twenty-three-year-old Joan Baez, to follow his lead. She performed Newton's hymn at the 1964 Newport Folk Festival and included it in the *Joan Baez Songbook,* published the same year.

By the late 1960s, "Amazing Grace" was becoming part of the pop secular culture. Woody Guthrie's son, Arlo, used it in his movie, *Alice's Restaurant,* and he hollered it out at the Woodstock Festival to a crowd that was less religious than stoned and muddy.

December 1970 was a crucial period for "Amazing Grace." In that month Judy Collins recorded her a cappella version in St. Paul's Chapel at Columbia University.

Collins, at thirty-one, was no newcomer to religious music or celebrity. She had sung "Amazing Grace" as a child in church choirs. Her mother's Tennessee family included ministers and missionaries.

As a participant in civil rights marches and rallies, she had often performed the hymn "as a rune to give magical protection—a charm to ward off danger."

Collins was burned out from constant touring, disconnected from friends, empty of spirit. Attempting to recover, she joined a New York City encounter group. One night, after a particularly rough emotional session with other participants, she asked them to stop and sing "Amazing Grace" with her. The effect was so electric that the next morning her producer, who was at the session, suggested that she record it. Seeking plain and unadorned sites for her recording—she first sang the Shakers' "Simple Gifts" in a Greenwich Village loft—she chose St. Paul's Chapel for "Amazing Grace," empty except for a choir of her friends, who hummed the second stanza as her background.

She used the by-now-standard version with Newton's first three stanzas and "10,000 years" as the fourth. But most significantly she altered the "I" and the singular voice in the third stanza to "we." She appealed to the entire country, indeed the world, well beyond the first-person voice. God's grace was not just for one soul.

Collins could not have anticipated what happened next. Suddenly this old hymn hit the pop singles charts. In a country besieged by a never-ending war in Vietnam, a wave of drugs, and the Manson murders, it struck home.

According to Turner's discography, there were hundreds of other recordings, among them the Royal Scots Dragoon Guards (bagpipes), Aretha Franklin (in the tradition of Mahalia Jackson), and Rod Stewart (a country-blues rendering). By the year 2000 more than one thousand albums included "Amazing Grace." Almost all of this was a result of Collins's recording.

Said Collins of those days: "I have a friend who says it changes the electromagnetic field; that it has the ability to transform the room into something different and better. It really is powerful."

That power has always been evident in the America that preserved and changed "Amazing Grace." It is the quintessential song for a nation of slaves and immigrants who know dangers, toils, and snares up close; where "wretch" is a term that resonates to many who remember the rags before their better days and where religious passion is bred in the bone.

Because "Amazing Grace" is easy on the details of Christian doctrine, it is possible to ignore the religious message and accept it instead as a hymn of universal hope, a narrative of confidence that somehow through grace we will all make it "home."

Such is the power of John Newton's vision in that storm at sea.

"Be Thou My Vision" is another great hymn about wonder. It comes to us from an anonymous Irish poem, "Rob tu mo bhoile, a Comdi cride," dating from about A.D. 700. The text was translated by Mary E. Byrne and included in the journal *Erin* (1905). The verse is by Eleanor Hull and appeared in *The Poem Book of the Gael* (1912).

This ancient prayer is also a world hymn. It can be sung with iron conviction by anybody of any denomination or religion.

I had long considered it for this book, but the real insistence that it appear here came from my sister, Ruth, who adopted Judaism three decades ago when she married her Jewish husband. I had not expected her to retain such a passion for a Protestant hymn from her long-ago childhood.

Here's why we both love "Be Thou My Vision." This hymn worships a universal God. It pleads that the singer not forget that God. The ultimate cry: Allow me to keep this vision of you.

Visions are hard to hang on to and harder to understand, as John Newton knew. Visions are beyond words, beyond even music, lost in wonder.

Such a vision changed my life with blinding force—and I use

BE THOU MY VISION

Ancient Irish
Tr. by Mary Byrne
Versified by Eleanor Hull

Leave us not I pray thee . . . . and thou mayest be to us instead of eyes.
— Numbers 10:31

SLANE
Traditional Irish Melody
Harmonization by David Evans

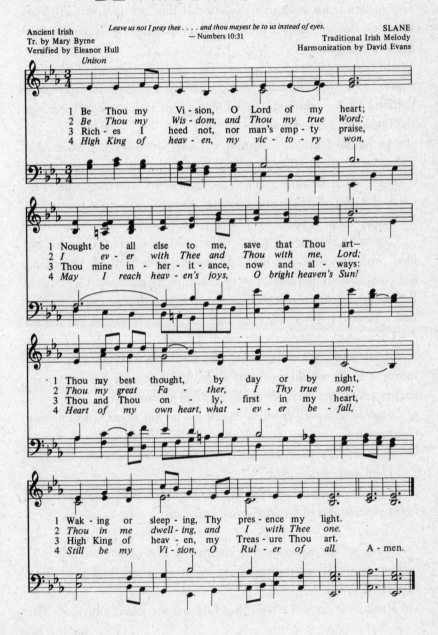

Unison

1 Be Thou my Vi - sion, O Lord of my heart;
2 *Be Thou my Wis - dom, and Thou my true Word;*
3 Rich - es I heed not, nor man's emp - ty praise,
4 *High King of heav - en, my vic - to - ry won,*

1 Nought be all else to me, save that Thou art—
2 *I ev - er with Thee and Thou with me, Lord;*
3 Thou mine in - her - it - ance, now and al - ways:
4 *May I reach heav - en's joys, O bright heaven's Sun!*

1 Thou my best thought, by day or by night,
2 *Thou my great Fa - ther, I Thy true son;*
3 Thou and Thou on - ly, first in my heart,
4 *Heart of my own heart, what - ev - er be - fall,*

1 Wak - ing or sleep - ing, Thy pres - ence my light.
2 *Thou in me dwell - ing, and I with Thee one.*
3 High King of heav - en, my Treas - ure Thou art.
4 *Still be my Vi - sion, O Rul - er of all.* A - men.

the cliché deliberately, remembering Saul on the road to Damascus. So bright was his vision that it blinded him for days. Mine, of no historical note, fortunately left me enough eyesight to continue driving to a hospital.

· My vision overcame me on the road to Ellsworth, Maine—Route 15 north, to be exact. And, as the hymn mentions, it involved light to see by—the light that Quakers invite into their meetings, the Light that is the Divine.

In Maine I built our summer house with my bare hands. No power tools at all, I liked to brag. Just a hammer, handsaw, and a T-square. I was too impatient to install Sheetrock interior walls. I resisted the idea of taping and sanding Sheetrock to a fussy finish, so I nailed up real pine paneling. Manly country stuff.

It was on this paneling that my seven-year-old Holly banged her head with an awful wallop while bouncing on her bed. Days later she complained suddenly of an excruciating headache and we rushed her to the Island Medical Clinic, where the doctor tested her reflexes, flashed light in her eyes, and advised us to get an immediate CAT scan at the Ellsworth Hospital.

Annie and I placed her on the backseat. I was certain that at any moment Holly would die from a blood clot as we sped north over narrow blind-crested roads to the hospital an hour away.

I swore to myself if Holly died I would kill myself and take my chances on finding her again in the afterlife. By night, I, too, would be dead. Later, Annie told me she had planned the same for herself.

Then grace descended.

This was a word I had never thought about before. Grace. I had never experienced it, couldn't even define it.

Grace.

From nowhere, unsought, and inappropriately. My child was maybe dying. I was doing eighty miles an hour. And this thing happened.

I suddenly felt an enveloping love for the entire universe. Not just for my suffering child; for Annie. For all of it. For all our living and dying.

And I knew I was loved in return. From the very depth of the stars I was loved.

There would be no suicide, no matter what happened to Holly.

After the CAT scan, the doctor said Holly was OK, and Annie and I collapsed in thanks. A vision of love became palpable. Love had transcended Holly and Annie and me and infused every pebble on the road as we tore desperately toward Ellsworth. All the earth erupted in light.

It is hard for me to remember this story without tears. Once, a few glasses of wine into my dinner, I tried to tell my dining companion, a stranger I'd just met, a professor of psychology at MIT, about this vision.

"Were you raised in a religious home?" he asked, a bit skeptically, and let it drop, while I nodded and dabbed at my eyes with a napkin.

So much for my vision, I later realized he had implied. I'd just had a sudden memory of better times. God hadn't shown up in an illusory burst of grace. I had just regressed back home over five decades for one moment.

Grace, or memory, I don't care what my Ellsworth vision is filed as. It remains, years later, a vision of enormous significance to me. And if God didn't visit overwhelming love on me and my little family there, then God certainly drenched my mom and dad in grace, and all who came before them. So, somehow, God's grace was with us, despite the clinical dissent of the professor.

"Be Thou My Vision" is not a hymn about reason. It is about faith from the heart. Almost all of this poem is revealed in that first line, "O Lord of my heart" (unlike many contemporary poems where the meaning is secreted away until the last line).

Most important, this is not a Lord of dogma, not a three-in-one God; not a crucified one either: Jesus' name is never mentioned. Not the historical Jesus; not the present Jesus. No doctrine divides the singers. This is a hymn for the heart's vision.

Years ago, as a confident young rebel, I would have scoffed at what I just wrote. "Heart's vision"? Explain all that, I'd demand. Why do religious people escape into vague terms? People of faith really have no idea what they're talking about so they just drift off into nonsense. Define this word "vision," I'd have said.

Now that objection seems flat-out foolish. How absurd to demand a precise accounting for wonder.

A principal apologist for the vision of the heart is William James. In *The Varieties of Religious Experience* (1902), named the second most important nonfiction book of the twentieth century by a panel of Random House–appointed sages (*The Education of Henry Adams* was first), James recounts, among many such experiences, the visions of Dr. H. M. Bucke in a privately printed pamphlet at the turn of the century:

> I had spent the evening in a great city, with two friends, reading and discussing poetry and philosophy. We parted at midnight. I had a long drive in a hansom to my lodging. . . . All at once, without warning of any kind, I found myself wrapped in a flame-colored cloud. For an instant I thought of fire, an immense conflagration somewhere close by in that great city; the next, I knew that the fire was within myself. Directly afterward there came upon me a sense of exaltation, of immense joyousness accompanied or immediately followed by an intellectual illumination impossible to describe. Among other things, I did not merely come to believe, but I saw that the universe is not composed of dead matter, but is, on the contrary, a living Presence.

The vision extolled in "Be Thou My Vision" is also celebrated by Walt Whitman:

> I believed in you, my Soul . . .
> Loaf with me on the grass, loose the stop from your
> throat . . .
> Only the lull I like, the hum of your valved voice.
> I mind how once we lay, such a transparent summer morn-
> ing.
> Swiftly across and spread around me the peace and knowl-
> edge that pass all the argument of the earth,
> And I know that the hand of God is the promise of
> my own,
> And I know that the spirit of God is the brother of my
> own,
> And that all the men ever born are also my brothers and
> the women my sisters and lovers,
> And that a kelson of the creation is love.

Doris Grumbach recalls a personal vision in her memoir, *The Presence of Absence: On Prayers and an Epiphany* (1998):

> What happened was this: sitting there, almost squatting on those wooden steps, listening to the quiet, I was filled with a unique feeling of peace, an impression so intense that it seemed to expand into ineffable *joy*, a huge *delight*. (Even then I realized the hyperbole of these words but I could not escape them). It went on, second after second, so pervasive that it seemed to fill my entire body. I relaxed into it, luxuriated in it. Then, with no warning, and surely without preparation or ex-pectation, I knew what it was; for the seconds it lasted I felt, with a certainty I cannot account for, a sense of the presence God.

You cannot know how extraordinary this was unless you understand that I was a young woman without a history of belief, without a formal religion, or any faith at all. My philosophical bent was Marxist; I subscribed to the "opium of the people" theory. . . .

Until those inexpressible moments I had taken no notice of God. I had given His existence no attention, except to harbor a thoughtless conviction that God could not reasonably exist. When the sense of His presence had passed, my reason returned in the form of questions I asked myself until my family returned. But I went on for a long time mulling over the questions: How did I know who It was? Why did I so unhesitatingly give It the name of God? What did I need to do to get Him back?

Simone Weil, like Grumbach an unbeliever, had a similar experience. In 1937, this French philosopher, student of the classics, and factory worker, had read no mystical works, had never prayed. At twenty-seven, her life had been a long ordeal of migraine headaches, sinus infections, and pain. In the twelfth-century Romanesque chapel of Santa Marie degli Angeli where St. Francis prayed, "Something stronger than I was compelled me for the first time in my life to go down on my knees." She, too, experienced the sense of inexplicable visitation by an unseen, unknown Presence.

There are countless such stories of visions in the history of all religions, but as "Be Thou My Vision" cries out, they too often fade and we are left in the humdrum everyday, longing for their return.

The music of this hymn, like that of "Amazing Grace," offers no frills or tricks. "Slane" is an Irish ballad named for Slane, a hill near Tara, Ireland. In the fifth century at Slane the first fires of Easter were said to have been lighted by St. Patrick as a challenge to King Laoghaire. The tune was included in Patrick W. Joyce's *Old Irish Folk Music and Songs* (1901). "Slane" is honest and direct, elemental, plodding, like an ox in the field with a job to do.

From thirteen hundred years ago, the lyrics of this hymn that a child might have composed, deliver an unclever slap at clever modern times: "Nought be all else to me, save that Thou art"—that line leaves us with an awful lot of noughts in our busy, acquiring lives. We work to buy stuff and then return to work so we can buy even more stuff, and so on, until life is gone. For this we are saluted in the media for our "busy lifestyles," and we are rewarded with gadgets and goodies from instant food to electronic organizers to help us survive this exciting style of life. The emptiness of all this should be apparent, but for some reason, it is not. "Nought," the hymn reminds us.

Easy for the poet to proclaim in A.D. 700, when commercial temptations were few, we might object. No radio or TV or Internet to persuade him he is just a consumer whose mission is to consume. The word "shopping" hadn't been invented and neither had "career." All a man had to do was build shelter, put bread on the table, and tend sheep.

But even he had his busynesses, his worries to pry him from his vision of God's wonder. Life for him was probably nasty, brutish, and brief. But across time he speaks to us, asks that we extract ourselves from constant mundane nonsense and let God be our "best thought," our "wisdom," our "true word."

The third verse is quite specific about what is "Nought"—"riches" and vain "empty praise." It adds a value drawn out over four rising notes, "inheritance." And here the modern singer might want to stop and think about the impact of "inheritance." Such a mighty word, yet it almost sneaks by us as we move on to "now and always."

The poet reminds us of all that it has taken to get us here. He honors those who kept the faith, the simple faith in God, in the hard years before.

A few miles from the Rockbound Chapel in Deer Isle, Maine, is a little cemetery lost in the woods. While hiking one day, my family discovered the tombstones of John Toothacker and his wife, Elizabeth, who died after the Civil War; surrounding them the five small stones of their young children, Mary, James, Thomas, Abigail, and Edward, all dead in the same year, 1834, from some nameless disease. Yet on all of the tombstones were messages of faith.

I can't even begin to imagine what vision it took to sustain that mother and father through such a year. There was no talk therapy in 1834, no Prozac; nothing but a faith that all this horror had to mean something, somewhere, somehow. We inherit that faith, and if we neglect it, we dishonor those two parents and millions of people before us.

Today we seem anxious to get rid of our heritage, even the past of a few decades ago. We are taught by the digerati that speed is all, since the race for riches goes to the swiftest. We worship at the church of what's-happening-now. We invest in faxes, e-mails, Internet connections—whatever supplies instant information. And of course, as Thoreau warned us, machines drive us, not the other way around. We hurry here and there, with little time to remember. Pondering our inheritance seems so, well, ponderous.

And similarly, we have less time for family and also little occasion to recall our own personal inheritances. The simple faith of my parents, for instance, might seem quite out of date, not worth considering in the overheated information age.

And of course, living in fast times, it is easy to forget and ignore our personal visions. Not all of us may have been brought to our knees like Simone Weil, or struck blind like St. Paul, but in many lives are moments of insight—a bright light—that is our personal inheritance.

I have kept journals since I was sixteen, and in the very first one, while struggling with new ideas like agnosticism, atheism, transcendentalism, pragmatism, and a host of other isms, I cried out on the page: "Never forget God!"

In high school, on one of those standardized personality tests that were becoming popular—soon to evolve regrettably to the ubiquitous SAT inventories of useless statistics—I ranked "To know God and do His will" as what I wanted most from life as an adult. But soon that vision faded, as I decided it was Truth that I longed for, and also to become a published writer. I wanted to be noticed, to impress girls most of all. I planned to have my first short story published in *Esquire* by the time I was eighteen, and then a great American novel by twenty-one, and on and on—the usual adolescent visions of grandeur, which left God buried in the hopelessly out-of-date church. My mother, upon hearing these various announcements, regarded me quietly, patiently. My father said nothing.

Years later, in the little church down the road on Long Island, I found that lost vision again in a blizzard and a snowbound congregation. And again, on the road to Ellsworth, Maine, and yet again, as I relate later, before cancer surgery.

"Be Thou My Vision" in its ancient refusal to be clever, in its prayer that faith not leave us, and most important, in its depiction of God without doctrinal trappings, is a hymn for every person, of every time. That's why my sister, Ruth, loves it, and I do, too. It is a hymn beyond music and words, a prayer from the singer's heart, to God's heart.

Like John Newton and the anonymous poet of "Be Thou My Vision," I think it is best not to narrowly define the wonder of God. I am grateful for whatever vision the Infinite offers us.

One winter evening my wife and I ate dinner by the heat of the fireplace and afterward, as is our unfortunate habit now that Holly is off at college, we settled down in front of the TV to see if anything worth watching was on.

We clicked through a few channels and suddenly Billy Graham's son, Franklin, was preaching to us. I had heard that Franklin drove a mean motorcycle and led a wastrel's life for many years. But here he was, sounding and looking like his father, whom I had first seen as I sat next to Pop in that Ocean City, New Jersey, revival in 1948.

Billy was young then, brimming over with his message of Salvation and The End. At his sermon's conclusion, Billy pleaded that the unsaved in the audience raise their hands, come forward, and accept Jesus. To please my father, Billy, and God, I raised my hand, but was too timid to walk to the podium. To the tune of "Just As I Am, Without One Plea" sung softly by the choir, I was indeed saved, I hoped. What if Billy hadn't seen my hand?

Just to be sure, I repeated my vow at the Baptist Church's summer vacation Bible School the next day. In my bathing suit, after sandcastle-building period, I knelt on the sand, as directed by our teenage leader, and raised my hand again to heaven, as she instructed. One couldn't be too sure about these things. The consequences of not being saved were terribly grave, she informed us.

On the TV now, I remembered that "Just As I Am" would conclude the paid hour that Franklin Graham was hosting. This would be the same schedule that Pop and I had witnessed in 1948. Soon the replacement for the wonderful baritone of George Beverly Shea would sing "How Great Thou Art" and then Billy himself, if he were able, would deliver his carrot and stick routine, "Jesus loves you. Believe it or go to hell."

I assumed that George Beverly Shea was long dead and that Billy's voice would be a tape from an earlier meeting far in the past. He was in his eighties and ill, I had read.

Not so. There, in a packed Nashville stadium, we were about to see Billy live, and before him, George Beverly Shea, also live.

Shea's rendering of "How Great Thou Art" is forever burned into my memory. What a sonorous, soaring, confident hymn it is. And Shea's deep, sorrowful voice, tending almost to tears, much like Garrison Keillor's in tone, is one of the great dramatic instruments. There is profound wonder and worship in his singing, and I have no doubt that Shea believes every word he sings.

But this night he is indeed an old man, backed up by a choir to

HOW GREAT THOU ART

O STORE GUD   11.10.11.10 with refrain

Carl Gustav Boberg, 1885
English version: Stuart K. Hine, 1953

Swedish folk melody
Harm. Stuart K. Hine, 1949

1. O   Lord   my   God!   when I   in awe-some won - der   Con - sid - er
2. When through the   woods and for - est glades I   wan - der   And hear the

all   the *worlds Thy hands have   made,   I   see the   stars,   I
birds   sing sweet - ly   in   the   trees;   When I   look   down   from

hear the *roll - ing   thun - der,   Thy power through-out   the   u - ni - verse dis -
loft - y   moun-tain   gran - deur   And hear   the   brook   and feel the gen - tle

Refrain

played;   Then sings my   soul,   my   Sav - ior God, to   Thee,
breeze;

How great Thou   art,   how   great Thou art!   Then sings my   soul,   my

Sav - ior God, to   Thee,   How great Thou   art,   how great Thou art!

* Original English words were "works" and "mighty."

patch over his faded voice. Still, I hear him from the past in this eternal folk melody:

> O Lord my God, when I in awesome wonder
> Consider all the worlds Thy hands have made . . .

Sitting there on the couch, I sing along with him, as my wife regards me quizzically.

I love this music and I love George Beverly Shea's singing. But I find the lyrics impossible. The original text is by Carl Gustav Boberg, a Swede who lived from 1859 to 1940. It was written in 1885 after Boberg was caught in a violent midday thunderstorm, followed by bright sun and twittering birds. He reportedly fell to his knees in humble adoration and soon thereafter wrote a nine-stanza poem, "O Store Gud," which was published in 1891.

The lyrics were later translated into German and then into English by Reverend E. Gustav Johnson as "O Mighty God, When I Behold the Wonder," and soon into Russian, too. Stuart Wesley Keene Hine, a missionary to Russia, adapted the poem into four stanzas just before World War II, and the Billy Graham Evangelistic Team popularized it in the decades that followed. Graham did for this hymn what the international barnstorming team of preacher Dwight L. Moody and Ira D. Sankey did for "Amazing Grace" in the previous century. In 1974, "How Great Thou Art" was voted the most popular hymn in America by readers of *Christian Herald* magazine.

My mother appreciated these lyrics, overruling her grumpy son. Like Wordsworth, she loved nature's beauties—soaring sunrises, puffy clouds—and ignored black flies, earthquakes, tornadoes, berserk viruses. She, like the composer, translators, and adapters of this song, saw only God's goodness in nature: the birds singing "sweetly in the trees," "the brook, the gentle breeze."

I look at the universe and see similar pleasantries and also horrendous chaos and suffering. Thousands of innocents dying of curable and incurable diseases as I write these words; immense natural disasters that have nothing to do with sinful man, that can be ascribed only to the God this hymn worships. I cannot sing to the idea of a God who controls this sort of world, who indeed made it up. My God is elsewhere—in love, wonder, simplicity, and silence.

In the final verses, resonating with me for decades in Shea's baritone, we hear the old, old story of a God who could think of no other way to tell people he loved them than by allowing the torturing and slaughtering of His only son. Such a God I worry about; I do not worship.

And finally this hymn loses me in its last verse about the Second (third) Coming: "Christ shall come with shouts of acclamation." And of course, the sinners get theirs and the happy believers are whisked Upstairs.

I don't need this God. As I said earlier, I would take no joy of any sort in a vicarious revenge on infidels. If this is to happen, I don't want Jesus to come yet again.

I see Jesus here now with us, in the eyes of everybody I meet. The Shakers knew that, and John Newton learned to witness living grace everywhere.

So the lyrics lose me. I sing the words for old time's sake; for my dad and me there on the folding chairs among the potted palms next to the ocean over fifty years ago; I sing in memory of the new young man my dad admired—Billy of the chiseled jaw, the wavy hair.

And suddenly, he is there again on the TV, Billy reborn, a bit slower of gesture, not quite so much bounce to his patter, but the same act. Jesus is coming again, tonight may be the last chance you get to enter heaven or descend to hell. He tells a tale of a healthy man who dies unexpectedly, unsaved, much like the story of the unredeemed pagan who died in a crash of his sports car with which he had regaled my dad and me. And then, of course, to the thousands of people there, Billy calls for conversion right now, and then the raised hands and the march of the sinners from their seats to the altar as the choir softly sings "Just As I Am Without One Plea," another hymn that can bring me to tears of remembrance. Its effect on the audience is immense, even as it hit me as a child.

Few hymns encapsulate the born-again experience as "Just As I Am" does . . . at least that sudden born-again phenomenon. After Billy's passion, it's time to give it all up to Jesus. No more excuses or hesitation. No "plea." The sinner walks forward, kneels, and surrenders to the Lord of love.

My problems, as usual: the "lamb" business. The "blood shed for me." In these lyrics I see what Paul and the early Christians had envisioned in attempting to salvage belief out of the crucifixion disaster. To Paul, the crucifixion wasn't the end, really, not so shameful or devastating. You see, it was like those doves and, yes, the lambs that were butchered as sacrifices for Jewish sins every day at the Temple, turning it into a blood-soaked abattoir. The crucifixion was God's own sacrifice for the sins of His people. You couldn't expect Him to just buy a bird or a dumb animal. This is God, after all. So His own son will have to serve. That's it—God kills His child, just as Abraham almost did to Isaac. It's a tradition, you see. The crucifixion was not the finish of the mission. No, it was the beginning, a new covenant in blood.

But I can't buy that. Jesus died for you and me. Sure. I believe that. He died because He wanted to restore a vision of God—Love—not rites. Love. And because this was such a radical idea, and throngs clamored for Him and couldn't get enough of Him, he was executed like any ordinary rabble-rouser who threatened the religious establishment and Roman authority.

He was crucified then, and crucified time and time again for over two thousand years by the politicians and clerics of the moment. A beautiful dreamer, slaughtered. It happens all the time. A man who loves me, you, all the people who ever lived, live now, or will live. Trouble for those in charge, or an opportunity for cynical advantage as we have recently witnessed in Washington.

But there's really no need for this bloody lamb metaphor. I can't sing about that. I can't turn Jesus into a butchered animal. He is much more to me than that.

So, sadly, "How Great Thou Art" and "Just As I Am, Without One Plea" are filed in my mind as mere nostalgia for a magic time long ago at the seashore with my pop, who knew all the answers and was showing them to me.

My wife is relieved that I'm not buying Billy's story. She worries sometimes that I might suddenly become born again and rush off to join a cult of some sort. But I tell her, and myself, that I *am* born again. I have been since I was a child and raised my hand at Billy's original invitation, while the waves rushed in and out under the boardwalk. Jesus is the Lord of love, and knowing that, and trying to remember it day to day, is what being born again means to me.

The program ends. It may be one of Billy's last revival meetings. He is frail and seldom leaves his home, and it is obvious that George Beverly Shea will not be singing much longer.

I wish Billy had changed his routine a bit. After half a century it all seems a little canned. I remember a few years before when David Frost interviewed him on TV about the Oklahoma City bombing.

"Why?" Frost asked. "Why does God allow such things?"

Billy just shook his head. "I don't know," he admitted. "I don't know."

I liked that about the new Billy. The uncertainty, the refusal to make easy pronouncements: "God moves in mysterious ways" or some such cop-out. But Billy kept quiet.

Then he and Frost knelt in the studio and held hands while Billy prayed a simple prayer, humble in the midst of unknown wonder.

I love that man. I always have.

That he is fallible, I have no doubt. But of all the evangelists I have seen in action—from Carl McIntire to Jimmy Swaggart to Tammy and Jim Bakker—only Billy walks the worship he talks. Or tries to.

I just can't sing his songs all the way through anymore. But I sure can hum the tune, and remember the way it used to be.

IV

The Prayer of St. Francis

SONGS OF LOVE

MAKE ME A
CHANNEL OF YOUR PEACE

Verses 1, 2, 4

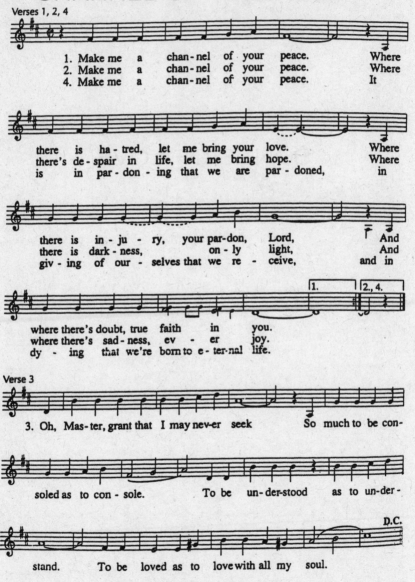

1. Make me a chan-nel of your peace. Where
2. Make me a chan-nel of your peace. Where
4. Make me a chan-nel of your peace. It

there is ha-tred, let me bring your love. Where
there's de-spair in life, let me bring hope. Where
is in par-don-ing that we are par-doned, in

there is in-ju-ry, your par-don, Lord, And
there is dark-ness, on-ly light, And
giv-ing of our-selves that we re-ceive, and in

1. where there's doubt, true faith in you.
2., 4. where there's sad-ness, ev-er joy.
dy-ing that we're born to e-ter-nal life.

Verse 3

3. Oh, Mas-ter, grant that I may nev-er seek So much to be con-

soled as to con-sole. To be un-der-stood as to un-der-

D.C.
stand. To be loved as to love with all my soul.

My brief Shaker gift that night—the dream I remembered as "It's so simple, so plain to see"—is very much like the gift of praying and singing "Make Me a Channel of Your Peace" with words attributed to St. Francis.

I find this hymn totally persuasive. If we can glimpse eternal life, if we can even guess at what Jesus envisioned, it's all here. And yet no hymn could be more antithetical to modern minds: To find your life you must lose it.

That leaves most of us dumbfounded. We have been taught from kindergarten that we must strive mightily for ourselves, for fabulous report cards ("plays well with others" will do for ethical concerns), high SAT scores, the most prestigious colleges, and later, top salaries, hot cars, and giant houses to show us off. We worship strivers. Our real expectation of eternal life is an endowment or a building with our name on it.

St. Francis teaches us the opposite. And a nagging voice, in even the most super-consuming and self-advertising of us, knows he's right.

One of the most remembered hymns from the funeral of Princess Diana was this one. It was her favorite, and its impact was tremendous. Diana was mourned not for her enormous (and un-earned) wealth, but for what she contributed, in her charities and most of all in herself.

During the mourning for Diana, a vision of eternity emerged—that vision that makes the most sense, oddly—irrational and rational at the same time. She lost her life and was loved by many because before her death she gave it away. That love, for a brief time, transformed England.

This prayer has been translated or set to music many times. My new *The Presbyterian Hymnal* (1990) and current Episcopal hymnals reprint the notes of "Dickenson College" composed by Lee Hastings Bristol in 1962 with a paraphrase of the St. Francis prayer by James Quinn. The previous Presbyterian hymnal included the music of Oliver Dungan, arranged by Fred Bock.

But to me, the most satisfying interpretation is in the Catholic hymnal *Gather Comprehensive* (1994), with words and music adapted by Sebastian Temple—the same version sung at Princess Diana's funeral by the choir at Westminster Abbey. Temple obviously understands the prayer's quiet dignity. Born in South Africa in 1928, he later became a lay Franciscan and composed many pieces for worship. His music does not intrude on the lyrics and overwhelm what St. Francis is said to have prayed. These are simple notes, simple but profound.

In all versions the words remain essentially the same. However, a translator's argument seems to be in progress in the first line. "Make me a channel." Others say, instead of "channel," "instrument" or "servant." I prefer "channel," which except for its unfortunate echo of the channeling craze is about right. "Instrument" is OK but "servant" implies somebody who is forced to work, a wage slave. The singer here, in St. Francis's thought, wants to give, is not forced to.

A contradiction also arises in verse three when some modern translations erase "Oh, Master" for "O Spirit." This is not a spirit St. Francis prays to. It's Jesus, the embodiment of that spirit. And I think we should honor that. It's what St. Francis had in mind, although I, too, often prefer that we widen our idea of God to include what is beyond the usual clichés of "organized religion."

The Lee Hasting Bristol version substitutes the pronoun "us" for "me"—as if the entire congregation is involved. Again, I want to stick with the original. The prayer is a personal plea, asking for personal responsibility. It's not a throng calling; it's one solitary soul begging to be released from the sin of self-love into heaven on earth and eternal life to come.

This hymn reminds me of a song in the play *Man of La Mancha*—"Dream the impossible dream." For St. Francis is asking to be allowed to do impossible things: to give love, forgiveness, faith, hope, light, joy, in place of the opposites: hate, injury, doubt, despair, darkness, sadness.

Most of us can barely manage to give these gifts to ourselves let alone to others with any consistency. As sinners, a word too often out of style in today's churches and utterly baffling to the secular world beyond, we struggle to attain these virtues. Channeling them to others is still another task.

Verse three is a real problem. Like Johnny Appleseed, we have been asked to plant goodness wherever we bustle, but now St. Francis asks that we forget our own pain and loneliness, that we console, rather than be consoled, that we understand rather than be understood, and love rather than be loved, and finally, in verse four, that we forgive before asking to be forgiven.

We are now light-years away from the contemporary temperament. Our age has been Donald Trumped. If you want attention, demand it. Aggrandize yourself—on your résumé, in your neighborhood, in your business, and especially in your own mind. Consolation for others? A fruit basket will do. Love? Understanding? Who has the time? Just so others get what *I'm* all about.

Church members are just as guilty as anybody else. The most difficult sermon topic of all, as I mentioned, is Jesus' observation that it is easier for a camel to pass through the eye of a needle than for a rich man to enter heaven. (And by heaven, I understand Him to mean heaven on earth, as well as heaven later.) I've heard all sorts of wriggling about that eye of a needle line. Didn't He really mean a certain canyon pass in ancient Israel? Wasn't the way therefore a little

wider? Say, big enough for me and my Lexus SUV? Let's be reason-
able here, some argue. It takes money to live—and lots of it. How
can I give oodles to the church if I don't make oodles?

And yet, the observation is rational. Stuff disappears. You and
your Lexus will expire. In relying on stuff and self as the center of
the world, you grasp only at death.

In each other we discover images of God, for we are children of
that God. In honoring each other we glimpse heaven right now.

The vision of "The Prayer of St. Francis" is the basis of the success of
Alcoholics Anonymous. Here we see proof of the rationality of the
irrational: Losing is finding.

AA's *Big Book,* published in 1939, has sold millions of copies.
In it, AA founder Bill W., a rum-ruined God-mocker, describes
how an old friend who had "got religion" convinced him to try self-
abnegation, to make up his own version of the Divine, and give
himself to that Divinity.

> I humbly offered myself to God, as I then understood Him,
> to do with me as He would. I placed myself unreservedly
> under His care and direction. I admitted for the first time
> that of myself I was nothing; that without Him I was
> lost. . . .
>
> Common sense would thus become uncommon sense. I
> was to sit quietly when in doubt, asking only for direction
> and strength to meet my problems as He would have me.
> Never was I to pray for myself, except as my requests bore
> on my usefulness to others. Then only might I expect to re-
> ceive. But that would be in great measure. . . .
>
> Simple, but not easy: a price had to be paid. It meant
> destruction of self-centeredness. I must turn in all things to
> the Father of Light who presides over us all.
>
> These were revolutionary and drastic proposals, but the

moment I fully accepted them, the effect was electric. There was a sense of victory, followed by such peace and serenity as I had never known. There was utter confidence. I felt lifted up, as though the great clean wind of a mountain top blew through and through. God comes to most men gradually, but His impact on me was sudden and profound.

St. Francis's mystical plea works. It's pragmatic. But the final line leaves us with a new mystery: "And in dying that we're born to eternal life." I have said earlier that to me heaven is right here, right now. But life after death? St. Francis obviously thinks there is more to come. What can this possibly mean? We have the Hallmark Card version, with angels strumming harps on a cloud; *The New Yorker* cartoon jokes, with St. Peter quizzing souls at the pearly gates on their virtues and sins; and we never lack for TV "sensitives" who talk to those who have "passed over."

Perhaps it might be best to think of eternal life as what it is not; not a *New York Times* obituary, not a book selected for the canon of English literature; not a boulevard named for you. Eternal life, as I understand "The Prayer of St. Francis," is the enduring soul of all humanity. We experience that soul by surrendering the cobbled-together construct of ourselves to each other, to those living and to those to come and who came before us. The ego is a fraud.

Beyond that limited understanding I cannot reach. St. Francis saw what I can't see. But I trust him. I recognize his vision of immortality as true. And so did many others.

Dostoevsky: "If you were to destroy in mankind the belief in immortality, not only love but every living force maintaining the life of the world would at once be dried up."

Spinoza: "We feel and know that we are eternal."

Rousseau: "Not all the subtleties of metaphysics can make me doubt a moment of the immortality of the soul, and of a beneficent providence. I feel it, I believe it, I desire it, I hope it, and will defend it to my last breath."

Edward Young: "Seems it strange that thou shouldst live forever? Is it less strange that thou shouldst live at all? This is a miracle; and that no more."

When my mother was dying, she had the faith of St. Francis. For twelve years she fought cancer, which started out in a breast when she was sixty. For all those years she never questioned her God, never doubted that heaven awaited her, and never stopped giving herself to her three children, to her job teaching math at the local high school (where she was many times voted "teacher of the year" by the student body), to her deacon duties at church, to her volunteer work visiting shut-ins for Meals on Wheels. She gave and gave, and her thirty-plus-year-old son in New York City, full of himself, didn't understand until years later what she knew.

For the three weeks that she lay dying in the suburban Philadelphia hospital room, I kept notes in my journal by her bedside, hoping in words to grant her my bogus notion of immortality.

In the journal I wondered where Mom's bravery and kindness came from so close to death. If from God, then I vowed to believe in God that second. At the time I wanted to make her a deity: she, whom I had so often criticized for her perpetual giving of herself. She had given away her entire self, complained the young man-about-town in an earlier journal.

But now I saw beside me real courage, love, and faith that never doubted. In those last three weeks of her dying, I learned true immortality.

I wrote my notes furtively with a Bic pen, my journal on my lap, when I thought she was sleeping. In my scribbling I participated in her strength, even as a biographer draws power from a good subject. She wouldn't understand this paper honor, I knew—this private proclamation of mine.

Mom honored people by deeds, not notes. She didn't preach or spin morality tales. Her lived life was her message. Her theory of a sacred being was the person in front of her. Death was but a passage.

Years later—when I was diagnosed with the same disease that

killed her—I would begin to know what she knew. What St. Francis knew. And I needed constant reminding.

Like John Newton's hymn, "Make Me a Channel of Your Peace" *is* the life of St. Francis. Attention should be paid to the details of that life, familiar to many.

Francesco Giovanni Bernardone was born in either 1181 or 1182 in Assisi, Italy. Like the date of his birth, many of the particulars of his life are uncertain. Story, myth, and church propaganda fill in the blanks. He wrote little but his spirit survives, if not his particulars.

The political and economic atmosphere of Assisi at that time was not unlike our own. Money—a new and popular method of exchange—was becoming king. The other kings—the German emperor and the lord pope—were in a constant power struggle, as were the classes: a fading feudal aristocracy, knights looking for something to do, a new and bumptious middle class.

Towns and cities were at each other's throats. Assisi and nearby Perugia battled often.

Francesco's mother, Pica, a devout lady, had him baptized Giovanni after St. John the Baptist, but his father, Pietro, a textile merchant who specialized in high-end fashions for Assisi's wealthy, insisted he be called Francesco, in honor of the French, whom he admired for their flair. So Francesco it was.

When not involved in war—civil or otherwise—Assisi was an energetic, frequently faithful, just as frequently libertine, town of twenty-two thousand. It was built on the buried Roman and Etruscan cities it replaced. Santa Maria Maggiore, the first cathedral, rose on the ruins of the temple of Apollo.

Behind the commercial hubbub was another city; more than a third of the population was poor and 10 percent lived in squalor. Mobs of beggars prowled the streets, and just outside the walls, lepers lived as outcasts in their lazarettos. They roamed the countryside shaking their rattles and clappers, as required by law, to warn of their approach. Popular theology had it that the lepers, with their disease, paid for their sins or the sins of their families.

Young Francesco, sheltered and doted upon by his parents, seemed unaffected by misery. According to *The Legend of the Three Companions,* "Francis grew up quick and clever, and he followed in his father's footsteps by becoming a merchant. In business, however, he was very different from Pietro, being far more high-spirited and open-handed. He was also intent on games and songs; and day and night he roamed the city of Assisi with companions his own age. He was a spendthrift, and all that he earned went into dining and carousing with his friends. . . . In all things Francis was lavish, and he spent much more on his clothes than was warranted by his social status."

Francis, the clotheshorse, was also remarkable for his sweetness and cheerfulness. At any moment he'd launch into a song he had picked up from roaming troubadours and minstrels, mostly in French. Whenever moved, Francis usually switched to French.

He had all that a fifteen-year-old eldest son might want, roistering male friends, ready girls, and deep pockets. He showered money on innkeepers and beggars with abandon.

But his was not a generosity inspired by compassion. To Francis, it was expected of him, a noble in the making. Part of his adolescent game plan was to attain high rank through the glory of war. Francis would become a knight.

At the time there were any number of causes enabling one to become a knight. In 1200 the common people of Assisi, the *homines populi,* including the new merchant class, rebelled against the well-born wealthy, the *boni homine.* Most of the ancient nobility fled to Perugia, as their houses and castles were demolished by the mob.

Not long after, Perugia declared war on Assisi, and Francis was among the troops marching out to meet their army, but not just as a foot soldier. When Assisi's forces mustered in December 1202, he mingled with the knights in front of the cathedral of Santa Maria Maggiore.

It was a gala and festive occasion. The infantry marched at the head of the parade out of Assisi, behind the banners of various town quarters, then came the knights with Francis astride his fine horse, followed by the *carroccio,* a fancy wagon pulled by white oxen and displaying an altar of lighted candles and a jeweled crucifix, where priests celebrated Mass.

Francis, wonderfully decked out in fancy armor paid for by his father, pranced the four hours to the battle site, expecting a swift victory. This was not to be. In short order Assisi's troops, and Francis, were in a panicked retreat, scattered into the woods and fields and decimated by the pursuing Perugians.

That might have been the last to be heard of Francis, except that he had a terrific horse and a noble attitude. Perhaps he was useful for ransom. Instead of being butchered, he was locked up in a Perugian dungeon for a year—where his health was nearly ruined—until his father paid the ransom price. Francis returned home to the textile trade and a gradual recovery. He was twenty-two.

After a year or so clerking at his father's store, he announced plans to join a crusade to liberate the Holy Land—one of many that set out during this period, usually with dismal results. Once again, his father spared no expense in providing his son with the best armor, another regal horse, plus a squire to carry his shield, and a magnificent cloak to throw over Francis's shoulders

And so Francis set out for his second try at martial renown. But only a few hours from Assisi, he met a bedraggled knight on the road, limping, alone, horseless, in rags. Francis took pity on him and gave him his wonderful cloak.

That night he became ill and a voice asked him what he thought he was doing.

"What do you wish me to do, Lord?" asked Francis.

"Return to the land where you were born, and you will be told what you must do."

Back in Assisi, he fell into a limbo, attempting to recapture the hijinks of his youth, but losing interest. He was at a turning point— for himself, and also for the Church.

For hundreds of years the Church had been ruled by what Jacques Le Goff in his *Saint Francis of Assisi* terms a "terrorist language of the sacred." The people were passive, ground down by poverty and political and religious subjection.

But the faithful were in increasing turmoil. In 1184, the Waldensians, men and women lay workers, dedicated themselves to prayer, good works, Bible reading in the vernacular, and preaching outside church authority. Of special concern to the Church was the role of women in preaching—an abomination. The Waldensians, and a similar group, the Humiliates, were condemned as heretics.

Abroad, Saladin reconquered Jerusalem from the Christian forces in 1187 and a third and then a fourth crusade were launched to win back the Holy Land. Both failed. Still to come was the infamous Children's Crusade of 1212 that lured thousands of devoted youths from across Europe to death and slavery in the name of Jesus.

A more subtle challenge to official doctrine was the rising economic power of the towns. Money and the accumulation of material goods were worshipped as competing virtues. The Church's list of the Seven Deadly Sins, formerly led by Pride, was now headed by Avarice.

Many of the deadly sins festered inside the Church itself. Pope Innocent III (1198–1216) issued a stream of papal bulls against usury, gluttony, and sexual abuses by priests. The Church enjoyed stupendous wealth, but to many it was becoming a travesty. People fled in droves, searching for something better to believe in.

But for others, and for Francis all of his life, the Church, despite its failings, held the keys to the Kingdom of Heaven. Most important, it was there that the Eucharist was celebrated.

One day, perhaps escaping from his father's shop, Francis walked into the crumbling church of San Damiano. On the wall was a typical crucifix—Jesus, His arms outstretched in agony, as if asking for help. Such crucifixes were common in Assisi, so ubiquitous as to have become meaningless to Francis. But for some reason, perhaps because he was lost and ready to see for the first time, Francis suddenly realized what the crucifixion meant. This man had let Himself be nailed to the cross out of love for him—Francis, failed knight, bored playboy.

And then, according to legend, the crucifix spoke to him in that empty building: "Francis, repair My house," Jesus said.

Francis, in tears of astonishment, stumbled into the daylight with his first hint of a new direction: He'd use his masonry skills, learned while shoring up the stone ramparts of Assisi, and fix San Damiano. "House," to him, meant this particular house—not, so far, the larger Church.

Soon after, in his continuing quest, he decided to make a pilgrimage to Rome. Thomas of Celano tells us he borrowed a poor man's rags for the trip. In Rome he noticed the pittance donated by the wealthy at the collection box. He joined a group of beggars outside the church doors and witnessed the empty vanity of the rich and their loathing for sorts like him.

About this time, perhaps on his ride back to Assisi, Francis came upon a leper on the road. Valerie Martin, in her *Salvation,* imagines the scene. The leper asks for alms and Francis opens his purse and extracts a thin piece of silver:

> The old familiar reaction of disgust and nausea rises up, nearly choking him, but he battles it down. He can hear the rasp of the leper's diseased, difficult breath, rattling and wet. The war between Francesco's will and his reluctance overmasters him; he misses a step, recovers, then drops to one knee before the outstretched hand, which is hardly recognizable as a hand but is rather a lumpish, misshapen thing, the fingers so swollen and callused that they are hardly differentiated, the flesh as hard as an animal's rough paw. Carefully, Francesco places his coin in the open palm, where it glitters, hot and white. . . . Tenderly he takes the leper's hand, tenderly he brings it to his lips. . . .
>
> The two men clutch each other, their faces pressed close

together, their arms entwined. The sun beats down, the air is hot and still, yet they appear to be caught in a whirlwind. Their clothes whip about, the hair stands on end. They hold each other for dear life.

Thomas of Celano adds that when Francis is remounted on his horse and glances back at the leper to say farewell, he sees no one.

At the end of his life, Francis commented on this moment in his *Testament:* "This is how God inspired me, Brother Francis, to embark on a life of penance. When I was in sin, the sight of lepers nauseated me beyond measure, but then God Himself led me into their company, and I had pity on them . . . after that I did not wait long before leaving the world."

Francis returned to his job of repairing San Damiano. For this he needed money. On impulse—perhaps his father was in France on a business trip—Francis took a bolt of fine cloth, tossed it over his horse, and sold both cloth and horse in a nearby town. He hurried back to San Damiano with a bag of coins and presented it to the elderly priest in charge, explaining that it was his donation to the building fund. The priest, who knew Francis's father and his ferocious temper, declined the purse. Legend has it that Francis then hid in a cave for a month, supplied with bread and water by a friend, while his father searched the countryside for his thieving son.

What followed, if legend is correct, was one of the great father/son confrontations of history. The local bishop summoned Francis and his father to a public showdown in the town square. There, Francis tore off all his clothes, flung them and his ill-gotten purse at his father, and shouted to the crowd: "Listen, everyone! Listen! From now on I can say with complete freedom, 'Our Father who art in heaven.' Pietro Bernardone is no longer my father and I am giving him back not only his money but all my clothes as well."

The bishop took the naked Francis in his arms and wrapped him in his own cloak. His father left, with his purse but without his son, publicly humiliated.

Now dressed in common garb, Francis continued to repair not only San Damiano but other local churches, singing in French and praising God. What do you do when you have fallen in love with Love? He couldn't keep still. He helped out at the lepers' hospice and begged up and down the streets for donations of stone for his rebuilding projects.

People still regarded him as a madman or, at best, the insolent, ungrateful son of a long-suffering citizen, Pietro. But gradually they grew used to him. His old charms and laughter had not left him.

One day in an oak forest, he came upon a small, deserted chapel that belonged to the Benedictines, who called it Our Lady of Portiuncula, or "of the little benefice," an oratory for vinedressers and foresters.

Francis began his repairs. He vowed he would become a hermit here, worshipping God and seldom showing his face in town. To celebrate Mass, he invited a monk to visit who read a Gospel passage to the would-be hermit. Jesus commands his apostles: "Take no gold, nor silver, nor copper in your belts, no bag for your journey, nor two tunics, nor sandals nor a staff . . . and preach as you go saying, 'The Kingdom of Heaven is at hand.'"

Francis cried out: "That's what I want! This is what I desire with all my soul!"

He had heard these words all his life, but suddenly it was clear. He would be no hermit, shut away at Portiuncula. Like a knight with a new cause and new clothes, Francis would take to the road. His years of conversion were complete. Neither he nor the Church would ever be the same.

Francis fashioned a tunic out of rough cloth in the shape of a cross. His belt was an ordinary rope. On his feet, nothing. His vow: "To follow the naked Christ."

His message—delivered to whomsoever he met—was simple. The three great evils are power, wealth, and knowledge (fancy academic learning). He was a primitive Christian, trying to walk in

Christ's exact footprints. He cared not much for the Old Testament and everything for the New. To him, all that is required of us is a recognition of God's love and a constant meditation on that love. The ponderings of theologians are worthless.

Power—any domination by one person of another, however subtle—is anathema. Thus his followers became not an order, but a brotherhood, without leaders. No one was more important than another, and Francis considered himself the least of the least.

Francis preached that money was dirty. He refused to carry it or touch it; it inspired in him an almost physical revulsion. One day a follower left a bag of money in Portiuncula. A brother picked it up—perhaps it could be donated to the poor? Francis scolded him and forced him to bury the sack in donkey dung.

The same for property—Jesus owned nothing, neither should the brothers. Books, which were expensive, were banned, the Bible excepted. One might accumulate many books and pride oneself on a library, or on the false learning that books inspired.

To his sexually libertine neighbors and some priests and monks, Francis preached a strict chastity: all passion for God.

Permanent housing was forbidden. His brothers should live in temporary reed shelters, or a cave would do, or a room donated from someone outside the flock. "If we owned anything we should have to have weapons to protect ourselves . . . we are resolved to possess nothing temporal in this world."

What really resonates in our memory is that Sunday School illustration of St. Francis and the animals. He adored animals. It is said that animals recognized him as a saint before people did, and that they fled to him for refuge because they sensed that with him human wickedness couldn't touch them; that a hunted rabbit curled up against him; that birds perched on his shoulders and listened to his sermons; that the vicious wolf terrifying the town of Gubbio was tamed by his gentle words.

When my dog Lulu was diagnosed with cancer, about the same time I was, some people, including my oncologist, found my depression over her dying hard to understand. It's just a dog, I heard in their muted expressions of sympathy.

But to St. Francis Lulu was more than just a dog. He would have found it quite natural that I talked to her like a friend, since the first day I adopted her from the local animal shelter, where she had languished for over a year.

I told another friend, Rob McCall, the Congregational minister in Blue Hill, Maine, about our conversations. "We talk about important stuff, running on the beach, the weather, chasing sticks, and food. Lulu loves to eat, unfortunately just about anything."

"I'm sure you don't talk about theology then," Rob laughed.

"Nope, just important stuff."

Lulu was ninety pounds of shaggy mutt. In fact, her shelter name had been Chewy, after the hairy *Star Wars* character. She looked as if a committee had tacked her together, with a German shepherd face, floppy dreadlocked Airedale ears, and a Golden Retriever body. Her muzzle said ferocious, her eyes indicated kind, and her tail wagged like a puppy's for friend and stranger alike.

Our delight during our ten years together was the Long Island bay beaches in winter and the Maine woods in summer. Lulu, with her long coat, hated heat; she adored snow and ice. In January she'd plunge into the surf with a gigantic happy splash—and paddle past ice flows to retrieve sticks I had tossed.

In the summer, after a day curled under the cabin's porch to avoid the heat, she emerged at sunset for our ritual evening tennis ball game on our ridge road overlooking the sea and Acadia National Park. Until old age and cancer slowed her down, she chased balls into the twilight and then we both crashed in the grass and felt the darkness fall around us.

Lulu was unconditional love, God spelled backward. She would jump on the sofa when I seemed depressed, rest her head on my shoulder, and stay that way, or lick my hand until I told her enough already. When other dogs rushed up to us snarling and threatening, she calmed them with her steady gaze and firm but pacific stand.

Despite her German shepherd ancestry, she didn't know how to do violence. She loved to chase seagulls ("Clear the beach, Lulu," I'd call, and the mildly amused birds flew off lazily after her charge). But one day when we found a gull trapped in a mass of seaweed, Lulu had no idea how to proceed. Her fancied prey was helpless, inches from her jaws. But she just stared at the terrified bird until I freed it and it flew off.

Lulu and I were kids together. Like my spaniel mutt, Duke, who roamed my boyhood fields outside Philadelphia with me (now all suburban houses, swimming pools, and asphalt), Lulu and I pretended we were not aged eleven and sixty-three, that we would romp forever together. Or I pretended and Lulu just couldn't be bothered with age.

Our last hike in Maine was into a golden October valley over maroon blueberry fields to a secluded lake—the Frost Pond. Lulu swam and I just lay on the field and watched the clear sun-washed sky and wondered if anything would ever be this perfect again.

Lying in that field, I remembered St. Francis's hymn, "Canticle of the Creatures," or "The Song of Brother Sun," a vision of nature quite unlike that of his gloomy church. During his final days, suffering in his dark cell in Portiuncula, Francis summoned the brothers to listen to his final composition, later called the first great poem in the Italian venacular:

> Praised be you, my Lord, with all your creatures
> especially Sir Brother Sun
> through whom you give us the day and light
> he is beautiful, radiant with great splendor,
> and of you, most High, he is our symbol . . .
> Praised be you, my Lord for Sister Moon and the stars
> in heaven, you created them clear and precious and
>   beautiful.

> Praised be you, my Lord, for Brother Wind
> and for the air and for the clouds
> for the calm blue skies and for ever changing weather
> through them, you sustain life in all your creatures.

The spirit of St. Francis was with Lulu and me in those final months—old dog, aging man, chasing up and down hills and beaches for the sheer exuberance of it all.

One morning, only a few days before my surgery, St. Francis may have visited us in a more direct way. Lulu slept on the floor. I lay on the sunroom couch, tired, weak, apprehensive. Paul Sullivan, a friend from Maine, telephoned to wish me well and said that Reverend McCall had mentioned my name on the Sunday prayer list. After we said good-bye, the room filled with what I can only describe as a force, as if the air pressure had tripled. It wasn't a vision of light and love, but a sensation of universal power. I skeptically tried to explain it away as a mood of the moment brought on by the phone call but couldn't, and although I expected it to fade away immediately—and begged it not to—the presence lingered with me and Lulu for perhaps half an hour before gradually leaving.

It is easy to dismiss such accounts. We have read endless tales of Jesus or Mary or a saint appearing to true believers in a pizza pie crust or a wallpaper stain. But I cannot deny that force. Like the events on the Ellsworth road, it was unexpected and not requested. I needed comfort and assurance, not force. But force I got. Nothing gentle about it.

One of the most convincing visitations from the Thin Places in all of literature is that of novelist Reynolds Price in his classic memoir of cancer recovery *A Whole New Life*. Price's cancer, unlike mine, was exceedingly painful, a tumor that curled down his spine like a snake. He endured months of radiation therapy.

One morning, Price says, he fell into an exhausted sleep. He was transported to the shores of the Sea of Galilee. Jesus came toward him. Price called out to him about his pain, and chances for survival. Jesus said merely "Your sins are forgiven," and turned and walked away. Price complains to himself that his sins are not exactly what bother him at the moment. He asks Jesus about ending the pain, and would he live? Jesus says simply—"That too." And Price finds himself back in his room.

He did indeed survive, confined to a wheelchair. And he learned to manage the pain.

Price is quick to criticize his memory of this event. As a respected literary critic and essayist, he won't accept this as a piece of Hallmark card sentimentality. Perhaps his pain had driven him over the edge? No, he answers, this visit was real. Jesus did speak those six words. Not a vision, not a metaphor, not wishful thinking, not temporary insanity. No question. Real.

In the same way, I cannot question the force in my room—St. Francis, Jesus, The Holy Spirit, none of the above—it makes no difference. Something else had been with my dying dog and me that afternoon. Like Doris Grumbach and her Presence, I long for it to return.

Just after my surgery, I noticed that Lulu's chest on the right side had developed a mass—about the size of a child's football. A fatty deposit, I hoped. But it grew larger and Lulu began to slow down. No longer did she lead our beach walks, she lagged behind. And soon she couldn't swim for a stick, she just walked into the water and stood there, grateful for her old ocean friend, as if lost in nostalgia.

I took her to the vet, who did an inconclusive biopsy and put her on antibiotics to bring down a slight fever. I said I suspected she had cancer. When I mentioned my own recent operation, he remarked that it was not unusual for a pet and owner to develop the same disease.

Weeks later X-rays confirmed Lulu's massive breast tumor and another in her abdomen.

Lulu, like other dogs and cats I have had, wanted to die alone and hidden. Twice she ran off into the night after I had let her out to pee.

The first time, when she didn't respond to my constant calls, I worried that she had found a hole or shed to do her dying in, but at 2:00 A.M., suddenly she was standing outside the glass door, too weak to bark or scratch. I let her in with cries of welcome for a friend resurrected.

For a few days she showed signs of recovery, scrabbling into the car for rides to the beach, eating with customary vacuum-cleaner lust. But on the night of a March blizzard, three days before she died, she again ran off into the woods and ignored my calls. After midnight, Annie was shutting off the lights when she spotted Lulu standing in the snow motionless, coated with ice, a white ghost. Again we welcomed her back as if resurrected.

But in the nights ahead she could not sleep, panting constantly and moving from spot to spot every few minutes because of her pain.

On March 10, the date my father died, I took Lulu for her last trip to the vet, still uncertain about what to do. The vet said it was time. Lulu didn't notice the injection into her rump. She quietly lay down on a quilt while the doctor, nurse, and I patted her and told her how very loved she was.

Her death hit me like a horrible physical pain. I barely made it out of the vet's office, and on the way home I became a sobbing road menace.

For weeks I searched the animal shelters for a dog with Lulu's eyes. One day Holly spotted an animal adoption ad in the newspaper and said, "Look at this dog's eyes, Dad, so kind."

I adopted that dog, a Border collie mix with energy like a living spark. I named her St. Francis—Franny.

In the spring, Franny and I returned to Maine and the Frost Pond. I scattered Lulu's ashes along the shore of our last perfect day.

———

Here is Julian Green in *God's Fool,* describing the early days of Francis the street preacher:

> He was in love with God—and that wasn't all, because he went much too far, this madman with the lilting voice. He said that God was in love with us all; he would suddenly weep, weep for love, and some people would begin to weep, too. . . . People left their work, came out of their houses. One would think he had bewitched them and that he was going to make them leave this world to lead them straight to God.

Preaching his vision, Francis, the tramp, wandered the streets of Assisi frequently enduring insults. Unlike the pompous, bored priests who talked down to them with threats of purgatory and hell, Francis spoke in plain language, employing mime, song, and music, like a great actor or jester. The spirit was in this holy fool, and he was one of their own—Francis, son of Pietro, who had fought with the knights, toiled in his father's textile business, and misspent his youth. Now he preached of God's love for even the worst of them. He'd been there, too. He sang from his heart.

Gradually, over months, Francis assembled a band of brothers and, later, his first woman convert. A young noblewoman of Assisi, Chiara, inspired by Francis's sermons, escaped from her family home in the middle of the night with a friend, Pacifica. The two sought refuge with Francis at Portiuncula, where he cut their hair short and gave them basic garments like his own. He then hid them from the wrath of their families in local monasteries. Thus was born The Poor Ladies, later to be called The Poor Clares, vowing, like Francis, to follow a life of poverty, simplicity, and love.

Soon there were twelve brothers living at Portiuncula, all dressed in plain tunics with a cowl and a rope at the waist. Shoeless, purseless.

To Francis, they were not a new order like the Benedictines or Carthusians or Cistercians. They weren't exclusively lay people, either. Anybody could join his flock, including monks, priests, and the lord pope, if he wanted to. They walked along the road to Assisi, one behind the other, reciting their prayers, or they wandered in pairs begging and preaching repentance. Eventually they expanded their mission to other Italian towns and villages.

The Church, ever mindful of popular movements that might threaten its power, was starting to notice Francis. For his part, Francis dared to hope that the Church would give them its blessing.

In 1210 the flock journeyed to Rome in quest of an interview with the lord pope. Jacques Le Goff sets the scene in *Saint Francis of Assisi:*

> Innocent III was imbued with the pessimistic spirituality of the monastic tradition . . . the exact opposite of Francis' love for all creatures. . . . For Francis, enemies do not exist outside ourselves; they are our vices and sins, and in any case, one must not judge others. Innocent III saw the Church assailed by troops of enemies: the princes who called themselves Christians and on whom in turn (the Emperor, the King of France, the King of England) he declared excommunication and anathema; these heretics who were swarming . . . those Cathars and Albigensians, against whom he called for a crusade and prepared the Inquisition.

Now, to further ruin his day, this little, dirty fellow appeared before him and his luxurious and arrogant curia to preach this scandal—the living realization of the entire Gospel. The Church did not need yet another division, another order with another rule.

One version of what happened next is that Pope Innocent, despite Francis's eloquent presentation, pretended he was but a swineherd and dismissed him: "Go back to your pigs and preach all the sermons you want to them."

Legend recalls that Francis ran to a nearby pigsty, covered himself in dung, and returned to the pope, announcing: "Lord Pope, I have obeyed you with the pigs. Have the goodness to grant me what I request." Eventually the brothers were given oral—not written—permission to preach moral exhortations wherever they wished, as long as they pledged obedience to the pope.

Francis and his band left Rome officially recognized—sort of—and his fame spiraled upward. Soon there were a hundred brothers, then a thousand. By the chapter meeting of 1217, perhaps five thousand brothers (friars minor, as they preferred to be called) assembled at Portiuncula.

According to legend, in 1219 Francis traveled to Damietta, in the Nile delta, a town besieged by crusaders. His hope was to end the violence against Muslims by personally converting the sultan.

Francis discovered a motley mob of so-called Christians, more bent on theft than liberating the Holy Land. Soon this army was decimated by the sultan's forces and six thousand crusaders were killed.

Undeterred as battles raged around him, Francis set out on foot with a brother to find the sultan and chat about Jesus. At the city gate, soldiers arrested the pair and threatened to decapitate them. A Christian head was worth its weight in gold. Somehow, the ragged man talked his way out of this difficulty and inveigled an audience with the sultan. Because the sultan was a cultured, patient fellow, he did not martyr Francis on the spot for his gall. He seemed moved by his words, concluding, "I would convert to your religion, which is a beautiful one, but I cannot. Both of us would be slaughtered."

Francis accepted a safe-conduct letter from the sultan and promised to pray for his soul, as he had requested.

When the saint returned to Italy from his Holy Land trip, after a year's absence, he found his burgeoning brotherhood backsliding and spinning out of control. They lived in permanent housing and owned stuff. As yet, they had no officially sanctioned rule defining what they were supposed to be about. Francis was unwilling to ap-point superiors or to discipline mistakes. At the peak of his influence he was in danger of being assimilated, merged, and co-opted.

The Church stepped in. The pope realized the role that the friars could play in siphoning off heretical sympathies, if properly managed. And Francis, driven by a vital need to touch the divine body in the mystery of the Eucharist, did not directly challenge the pope. In *Mirror of Perfection* Francis explained: "Remember, my brothers, that the winning of souls is what pleases God most, and we can do this better by working with the clergy than in opposition. But if they obstruct the salvation of the people, vengeance belongs to God."

For the final six years of his life, Francis fought being absorbed by the Church, a losing battle.

When a final rule was approved by the pope in 1223, it had gutted the founder's vision. Most of the Gospel passages were omitted, the language was dry, legalistic, and stripped of poetry. Gone were the admonitions to care for lepers, love poverty, and rebel against unworthy leaders. Some possessions, books included, were permitted. Francis's paeans to the holiness of manual labor were muted. The right to preach was now reserved for a few of the elect, summoned by God and approved by bosses, not for all the brothers.

Too sick to protest, Francis secluded himself in hermitages for long periods, explaining, "Until the day of my death I will continue to teach my brothers by my example and my life."

When he died at Portiuncula on October 4, 1226, in agony, blind and covered with sores—some of them said to be stigmata from the crucified Christ—he was worshipped as a living saint. But by then he was more valued for his relics—bits of hair, teeth, and bone—than for his continued living.

In short order his body was buried in a sumptuous basilica that would have shamed him. He was promptly canonized and the Church ordered an official biography.

———

The Church used St. Francis, and continued to do so, to promote its own agenda. The "little black hen," as Francis described himself, who was in love with Lady Poverty and condemned power, property, and money, is now a "poster boy" for an institution too often enamored of all three.

But we remember him as one of the few people in Church history who loved all living beings without reservation, who followed Christ simply, without petty theology. And we adore him, too, for his former libertinism and frenzy for renown. We know Francis in our own time and person. No plaster saint this. He lives today as he lived eight hundred years ago.

The question remains: Did the man who composed "Canticle of the Creatures" also write "The Prayer of St. Francis"? In spirit definitely yes; in word-by-word detail, the evidence is unclear. Certainly the style of writing differs.

The historical evidence is this: The prayer first appeared in 1912 in a tiny religious journal called *La Clochette (The Little Bell)*, published in Paris by a Catholic group, La Ligue de la Sainte-Messe (The Holy Mass League), founded by a Father Esther Bouguerel (1855–1923). It was published anonymously as "A Beautiful Prayer to Say During the Mass."

A French marquis sent it (in French) to Pope Benedict XV in 1915. Soon it appeared (in Italian) in the Vatican's daily newspaper *L'Osservatore Romano*. About 1920, a French Franciscan priest printed it on the back of a card with the image of St. Francis on the other side, titled *"Prière pour la paix,"* but did not attribute it to St. Francis.

Between the two world wars, it circulated widely in Europe. A French Protestant movement, Les Chevaliers du Prince de la Paix, first assigned authorship to St. Francis. This claim was repeated in *Living Courageously* by Kirby Page, a Disciple of Christ minister in

New York City, and a social evangelist, pacifist, and editor, who also was the first to translate the prayer into English.

During the 1940s the prayer was always attributed to St. Francis, particularly in the books of New York's Cardinal Spellman.

In short, nobody really knows who wrote this prayer. But equally certain is that Francis, in his life, wrote it for us.

I don't recall that our family sang even the Presbyterian version of "Make Me a Channel of Your Peace" at church in the 1940s and 1950s. It is a new hymn to me, first heard while listening to a radio broadcast of Princess Diana's funeral and later as a before-dinner prayer at Paul Sullivan's house in Maine. I realized what a rebel yell it is, what a piece of contrarian logic.

And because my mother, in her quiet life, showed me the truth of it, I could understand and love this prayer the first time I heard it.

In church we sang other wonderful prayers of peace and healing and love and two that I still appreciate are "There Is a Balm in Gilead" and "Abide With Me."

It is difficult for our mostly all-white congregations to sing black spirituals without sounding clunky and ridiculous. We try to get into the swing of it and end up embarrassed. But with "There Is a Balm in Gilead"—Mahalia Jackson's favorite gospel song—we have a chance to sound not too self-conscious.

The hymn's easy rhythms and plain lyrics encourage us to envision a faraway place we know little about—Gilead, an area east of the Jordan River renowned for its healing plants. (Jeremiah 8 warns that all the medicine in Gilead will not heal the pains of the sinful Israelites.)

Gilead! What a fine word to hit hard in the singing, on the up-swing, as if we know what a marvelous and mysterious place this was

THERE IS A BALM
IN GILEAD

BALM IN GILEAD   7.6.7.6 with refrain

African-American spiritual
Arr. Melva W. Costen, 1989; alt.

and had, in fact, visited it. Gil-e-ad! Three syllables that lift the congregation. And right after Gilead another term meant to be belted out: "Sin-sick." I am reminded of the marvelous "wretch" in "Amazing Grace." "Sin-sick," oh, yes. And wounded.

The first verse is a first-person confession and the next two are third-person messages to others. This memoir/message is from one who is sin-sick, which in my theology means sick from lack of love: African, slave, alone in a country far from home, and later surrounded by hostile whites, unable to get justice or a decent education or find more than demeaning work.

For me, as a boy, there is a real memory of segregation even in the suburban North. My wife Annie, born in Alabama and raised in Mississippi, remembers it even more vividly. To varying degrees we both grew up in a world where we saw racial degradation forced on vast numbers of citizens.

Not that I knew what to do about it. In college, a few of my friends—the token blacks admitted there—participated in the first sit-in at a local Woolworth's luncheonette. I remember the assassination of Martin Luther King and all of us whites driving around with our headlights on in daylight to show we cared. I wonder now if our caring was partially a fear that a violent backlash might invade our suburbs.

And so the first words—"There is a balm"—so cool, so healing to the heat of injustice, then the line "sometimes I feel discouraged, and think my work's in vain" hit us hard. This is not a depressed WASP vice president burned out in his quest to become CEO; not a government bureaucrat bored behind his lifelong desk. This is a black American singing of work—janitor, maid, trash collector, cotton picker, whatever was allowed to him or her. Work deemed next to worthless. But the singer knows the dignity of that work, and is revived by the Holy Spirit.

I like the Holy Spirit in this hymn. Usually the idea of the Trinity, so neatly divided three ways by some theologians, makes me slam my hymnal shut. Some of these fellows dithered about how many angels can dance on the head of a pin and later figured out why segregation was a Christian principle for the Southern Baptists. It started with Cain and Abel, and what could be more logical than that black people, bearing the mark of Cain (pigment), should be subservient to whites?

Recently, the Southern Baptists apologized for centuries of close misreading of the Bible, and the suffering their theology caused. At the same time they affirmed that women should continue to be subservient to men in the household and may not be allowed to hold high church office. Another case of skewed reading of the Bible—Paul's letters: "Let your women keep silence in the churches: for it is not permitted unto them to speak; but they are commanded to be under obedience, as also saith the law" (1 Corinthians 14 v 34).

Yes, but where is the spirit of the law? We find it in this spiritual; not in petty theologians yanking verses out of the Bible.

I have no idea what spirit inspired the German Catholic Church to enslave ten thousand laborers during the Nazi years. I am sure there were biblical justifications. Cain and Abel again? Or just standard Catholic-inspired anti-Semitism? I note that in 2000 the German Catholic bishop agreed to pay twenty-two hundred dollars' compensation to each of those laborers, begging forgiveness for that bit of nastiness. In any case, only about one thousand were still alive. What a savings sixty years brought to the German Catholic Church!

I trust the theology of "There Is a Balm in Gilead." To me it's worth all the learned tomes over the centuries. I imagine that a tidy argument for the Trinity, the Triune God, the three-in-one, would be as incomprehensible to the creators of this hymn as it is to me.

Here I find honest words straight from the heart: "discouraged," "friend," "knowledge," and "tell." Anybody who professes to be a Christian like me knows in his gut what "discouraged" means here—at least my privileged, well-fed version of the word. Some days you wake up and it's all totally empty. Jesus, the Church, love, wonder, simplicity—none of it makes sense. Useless words.

For years, since I yelled down the stairs from my bedroom at my father, who was importuning his Thoreau-besotted, wise-guy, fifteen-year-old son to join him in church, as I had done for all of my childhood, I was far from any idea of the Holy Spirit. "I'm not going!" I yelled, and crushed him.

For decades I wandered in emptiness, "not going anywhere." Until the Holy Spirit—the spirit of holiness—revived my soul again. And I still constantly need revivals, resuscitations by that spirit.

Friend. "Jesus is your friend," counsels the singer in the second verse, and I sense that this is no angelic friend we are singing about, no business contact either, no cocktail buddy. This is a friend in every sense, somebody who loves you without qualification.

Knowledge. "If you lack for knowledge." Once again the hymn escapes the cliché of hundreds of other hymns. We expect the word "salvation" here. But we get "knowledge." Not college-knowledge, but the real thing. Not the learning of professors but deep-down wisdom.

Lend. "He'll not refuse to lend." Lend means a real transaction. To lend is to be a friend. When you are below dirt-poor, as the original singer-composers were, lending was crucial. It's what real neighbors do for each other. And it is also a slightly humorous idea—as in "lend me a cup of sugar," "lend me a dime." Something trivial. But in this case, knowledge is loaned. A sweet irony.

And finally, in the third verse, the word "tell": "You can tell the love of Jesus." Once again the hymn escapes the trite. Lesser efforts might encourage the singer to climb on a mountaintop and holler to the nations, or take up a cross and proclaim witness to the ages or similar bombast. Not here. Simply tell. Tell the love of Jesus.

"Tell" also because slaves were not allowed to assemble for worship—let alone preach. In 1845, in a typical southern ordinance, Georgia declared: "Negroes are not allowed to assemble under pretence of divine worship." The penalty was flogging or death.

"Tell," because the composers knew, even if legal, it is tough, indeed impossible to preach like Peter or pray like Paul. And, if you have faith, it really isn't necessary to mount a podium. The simple words of faith will suffice, however quietly spoken.

My shy pop wanted to preach, to convert his fellow General Electric workers in the low-voltage switch gear department. But I doubt if any of them ever knew he called himself a Christian. Speaking up, even telling, left him petrified. When guests arrived at our house, Pop headed to his basement workshop to tinker with a project and didn't reappear until they had left. Social situations confounded him. Even consumed as he was by the love of Jesus, he left the speaking up to Oral Roberts, Billy Graham, and Carl McIntire, sending them contributions and turning on the TV or radio only when one of them was preaching.

Once I asked Pop to tell me exactly what it was he believed. I wanted him to justify himself, without saying so directly. His reply was, "If you don't know, I can't tell you," and he walked away. He could not tell. But in his quiet way he showed me through his constant, if silent, kindness.

Prayer. Who indeed can "pray like Paul"? Not me. My father prayed constantly. He was kneeling in prayer at his bedside moments before he lay down and died in his sleep, without a symptom or a sound. A massive heart attack, said the doctors.

But I find it hard to address the infinite. In the morning, before working, I may kneel and call out the simple prayer I have cobbled together as the essence of what I believe: "God of love and wonder, grant me the grace to remember You today. Let me live my life as a prayer to You."

Then I shut up and listen for a hint of a reply, trying to still the constant hamsters on a treadmill that serve for my consciousness. I hope I have found the right words to describe the God I worship, and that He somehow matches my best guess about who He is, in whatever dimension of time or space or black hole He resides.

Even "God" is a word that is odd to me. I like the Native American term "Great Spirit," for it is the spirit of love and wonder that is huge in the human universe, the only universe I vaguely know, and soon shall leave. I assume that spirit is in the body and soul of every person I meet.

As Rick Moody states about prayer: "I don't know what it is, but it works."

At church I am sometimes asked to help out in the service by reading scripture and a few prayers. But I will not read prayers. I wonder why ministers, who often halfheartedly read prayers, don't worry that God will see into their souls and know these words are only lightly meant. They do not cry out, as a prayer should. Praying should involve the entire being, as it did my father. All of his prayers were from the heart. You are addressing the divine. How can we take that easily? I can't. Indeed, the whole process scares me.

I'd rather God talked to me when He felt like it. Just tapped me on the shoulder and said: Listen a minute, pay attention to this. Like a character in a Flannery O'Connor novel, far from holiness, but pursued by inevitable grace, I often feel unworthy, ignorant. Here, the hymn helps out. What can I know? Only "the love of Jesus."

The slave composer knows how hard it is to pray and preach. But you can simply tell the love of Jesus in both cases. How wonderful, how joyous, how absolutely right!

And finally, the singer leaves us with, "He died for us all." Once again there's none of the chatter about the Lamb of God, or a sacrifice of the only Son by a loving Father who just had to slaughter Him.

"There Is a Balm in Gilead" wants none of this God-slaughter. Too odd, too bloody, too utterly ridiculous for the slave-singers, perhaps. They had seen enough innocents slaughtered. "He died for all" is the simple concluding line. Of course Jesus died for all. He died because He loved people more than cheap theology. He died because He would not be silent about the corruption of established religion and empire; would not recant a word in the face of torture and death. He died for all of us, to show us something about God, about love. It's that simple. And this hymn knows it.

Dostoyevsky in his tale "The Grand Inquisitor," from *The Brothers Karamazov,* says this in another way. Jesus has returned to earth and has been captured by the established Church. The Grand Inquisitor tells Jesus He did His work a long time ago, but now He'd better not contradict modern Church doctrine, or He'll get another taste of the cross. Did Jesus have anything to say for Himself?

> The Inquisitor falls silent, he waits for a certain amount of time to hear what his Captive will say in response. He finds His silence difficult to bear. He has seen that the Prisoner has listened to him all this time with quiet emotion, gazing straight into his eyes, and evidently not wishing to raise any objection. The old man would like the Other to say something to him, even if it is bitter, terrible. But He suddenly draws near to the old man without saying anything and quietly kisses him on his bloodless, ninety-year-old lips. That is His only response.

That kiss is the balm in Gilead, and why I adore the simple honesty—the deep heart—of this brave slave hymn.

Millions of singers have confronted aging, dying—indeed the exact moment of death—with the words and melody of a quiet, profound, undemonstrative song, "Abide With Me."

Many other hymns are concerned with the afterlife, going to heaven to be with the Lord, earning a crown or a row of merit badges for a life well lived. But not many hymns—except "Swing Low Sweet Chariot" and the hymn version of the Twenty-third Psalm ("Yea, though I walk through the valley of the shadow of death . . .") and perhaps one or two others—dare to confront the final moments without triteness or bombast.

ABIDE WITH ME

And now, . . . abide in Him, that when He shall appear we may have confidence, and not be ashamed . . . — 1 John 2:28

Henry F. Lyte

EVENTIDE
William H. Monk

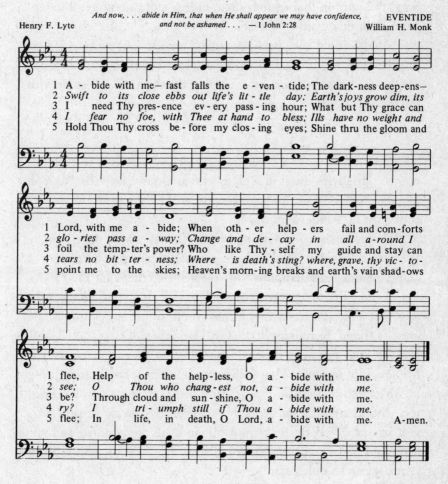

1 A - bide with me— fast falls the e - ven - tide; The dark-ness deep-ens—
2 *Swift to its close ebbs out life's lit - tle day; Earth's joys grow dim, its*
3 I need Thy pres-ence ev - ery pass - ing hour; What but Thy grace can
4 *I fear no foe, with Thee at hand to bless; Ills have no weight and*
5 Hold Thou Thy cross be - fore my clos - ing eyes; Shine thru the gloom and

1 Lord, with me a - bide; When oth - er help - ers fail and com-forts
2 *glo - ries pass a - way; Change and de - cay in all a-round I*
3 foil the temp-ter's power? Who like Thy-self my guide and stay can
4 *tears no bit - ter - ness; Where is death's sting? where, grave, thy vic - to-*
5 point me to the skies; Heaven's morn-ing breaks and earth's vain shad-ows

1 flee, Help of the help-less, O a - bide with me.
2 *see; O Thou who chang-est not, a - bide with me.*
3 be? Through cloud and sun-shine, O a - bide with me.
4 *ry? I tri - umph still if Thou a - bide with me.*
5 flee; In life, in death, O Lord, a - bide with me. A-men.

INNER PEACE

At the Rockbound Chapel, where many singers are of advancing age, "Abide With Me" is requested at almost every Thursday night hymn gathering. I think it is popular because it is so honest, and this honesty begins in that seldom-used, indeed almost obsolete and precisely right first word—"abide."

"Abide" could have been set aside by lyricist Henry Francis Lyte in 1847 for any number of stronger, more dogma-conscious terms like "save," but this hymn asks only that the spirit of God abide with the dying patient.

The definition of "abide" breaks so many ways: "to last, to endure," or "to continue to dwell in a place," or, as a transitive verb, "to look for, wait for," or even "to put up with." All meanings of "abide" are contained in "Abide With Me."

The singers ask for nothing but God's presence in the room, by the bed, as eventide falls and the darkness deepens. The patient is alone, nobody can help now. But there is no complaint here about illness and pain, no demand for extended life or a relief from loneliness, just a plea for a steady spiritual visit until the last closing of the eyes—a friend that abides in the finality that we all face.

The first two verses include fine lines of poetry: "Help of the helpless," for instance. That idea covers all of us, every human being in whatever situation, in excruciating pain, on death row, confined to a wheelchair, immobilized at home, or merely slowly passing away year by year. Nobody is cast out by God. All are honored and visited. And that spirit never leaves, doesn't just drop by with a bit of sympathy and a quick exit.

In the second verse, "life's little day" sums it up quietly and without cant. Life is indeed a little day and few hymns use language to such a good and precise purpose as "Abide With Me," at least in the first two verses.

The next two verses stumble into triteness now and then: "foe," "death's sting," "triumph," "victory." Often these verses reach for rhymes in a silly way—"the tempter's power" concocted to hook up with "passing hour," for instance, a real stretch for the otherwise un-obstructive rhyme scheme.

But the fifth verse evokes the moment of death without the usual chorus of angels; a simple light shining through the gloom points the sufferer to the skies and heaven's morning. The fact that heaven appears only once in a poem about death, and not until the last verse, is remarkable. This is not a song of easy comforts and all the usual phrases of the bliss to come for loyal Christians. It is humbly quiet and new, with tremendous integrity—and that's why we singers at the Rockbound Chapel request it over and over, Thursday to Thursday through the summer.

Some lines here proclaim an attitude toward aging and death that is the antithesis of our celebrated so-called "lifestyle." The lyrics do not celebrate change and worship "Thou who does not change." Only God is changeless—all else is fleeting.

Our culture does not value a changeless center. In fact, we wor-ship change and are made happy by a pop faith that proclaims, since all is change anyway, why not go down that river without resistance; indeed why not speed down it to stay ahead of those competing to exploit change for profit and celebrity?

Nowhere is this attitude more evident than in the hysteria for ever-new technology. The cyberspace cadets have concocted a new religion complete with a passel of techno-evangelists and their own special priestly lingo. According to them, the computer is the most stunning advance since the capture of fire. They preach that soon nothing will be the same. Their gospel rejoices that we are witness-ing the end of the human race. Soon we may be replaced by an electronic superbeing. Forward we all rush—toward we know not what.

The steady God of "Abide With Me" seems not to be present today. In fact, the enemy of progress is any notion of changelessness. A God whose world is without end—forget about it.

Our highest wish in the twenty-first century, often by people who call themselves Christians, is for a "pleasant lifestyle." "Style" itself is, of course, something that is expected to change.

But these were not the comforts of 1847 when Mr. Lyte wrote these lyrics. Comforts for the aging and dying at that time did not even include anesthesia, let alone mood improvers. We respect what comforts they had—real community, true friends, warm families— and if these were unavailable, then faith in a God who does not change, who abides.

Today, our "helpers" are blind insurance companies that refer to patients as "payment units" who are cared for by "providers," not doctors. Unless, of course, you are lucky enough to be part of an Amish or other religious society that will have nothing to do with medical insurance. There your community cares for you if you are sick. You have a name, and friends, and a soul—not a number.

"Abide With Me" is a hymn that perfectly describes the last moments of my kind, silent, and devoted father. All his life Pop refused to see doctors: "They are just practicing," he would joke. He asked Jesus to cure his illnesses, from a toothache to a double hernia. Each night he prayed by his bed for his family, his country, the world, and last of all, for himself. But Jesus responded only now and then, which was OK with Pop.

Finally, the night of his death, Jesus let him go gently. Pop left the light on for Mom, turned to that light, and when she found him an hour later, his face was one of utter peace.

Afterword

ONLY JOY

———

It gets dark and darker, and then Jesus is born.

—Wendell Berry

W̲hile I was writing this book, before my cancer was discovered, I tried to obey a note stuck to my typewriter: "Only Joy." That remains my motto, in writing, in life.

Since this is a book about hymns, not disease, I don't want to dwell on cancer; however, when I tell friends that the surgery, a radical mastectomy of the left breast, was one of the great spiritual moments of my life, they think I'm joking. But during my forty-eight hours in the hospital I felt no pain, only an abundance of love.

On the day of the operation, Annie and I walked about forty blocks to Memorial Sloan-Kettering hospital on Manhattan's Upper East Side. It was a stunning November day; fall had finally drifted down from Maine to New York. For a while we sat in a park near the hospital. Children on recess raced around us shouting and laughing in the falling leaves. To calm myself I repeated my friend Pat Strachan's advice—she had endured a cancer operation years before—"Just let them take care of you."

I checked in at the hospital and was greeted by unfailingly kind nurses, given a gown, and I walked into the operating room where my surgeon, Leslie Montgomery, who in her youth, beauty, and thoughtfulness reminded me of my daughter, Holly (I told her so), talked with me as her team did various things to my body. I went under laughing at the color-splattered cap of one assistant. "That's ridiculous," were my final words.

When I woke up in recovery, missing a left breast and some chest hair, Leslie was bending over me: "Your lymph nodes are clean, Mr. Henderson. Your prognosis is good."

"Hot shit!" I blurted, rather inappropriately.

The next two days were a storm of love. Friends I hadn't heard from in years and friends I didn't even know were friends telephoned with concern.

Holly called from Barcelona, where she was studying for a semester. She later wrote that she lit a candle for me in a small church by the Mediterranean shore. "Dad, I sat in the church for a little while, staring at the candle and listening to the private service for a family member who had passed away. For the candle I chose one of the many saints that spoke to me. The statue was of a man on his side, sleeping peacefully, with his shirt open, baring his chest. Two seashells covered each breast. It meant a lot to me."

In my semiprivate room, just to the other side of a curtain that divided us, a young man, Mark Harris, spent the night sleepless and throwing up, a stomach tumor. The next day, Mark's friends visited him and read Bible selections and prayed. Now and then Mark and I talked over the curtain and in the night I silently tried to send him some of the force of the presence that had visited me days before.

The idea of death became very real in that room, but so did the love that friends, doctors, and nurses brought to me and Mark. As Emily Dickinson wrote: "That love is all there is/Is all I know of love."

Love was all I had there. Ego was obliterated. "Self" seemed silly, a pasted-together mirage. The real was exactly what St. Francis said it is: "In the giving of ourselves we receive, and in dying we're born to eternal life."

Faith I didn't know I had, from my childhood, bred in the bone, carried me through those days of Lulu's dying and the long, often confusing and depressing months of consultations and treatment that followed.

Since I realized that "I" didn't even exist to start with, death became meaningless. "I" was free. We are all free. Joy resounds.

So many other grand old hymns might be celebrated here. Indeed we could compile an encyclopedia of joy just by listing those hymns that infuse congregations with peace, faith, and love, as well as others that are wonderful to sing for the melody alone, like "The Old Rugged Cross," words and music written by George Bennard of Reed City, Michigan, in 1913—the most popular hymn of the twentieth century. "On a hill far away stood an old rugged cross, the emblem of suffering and shame. And I love that old cross, where the dearest and best for a world of lost sinners was slain." In a few words, Bennard carries us back two thousand years to that hill and that cross.

Our encyclopedia of joy might include quiet songs like Will Thompson's (1847–1909) "Softly and Tenderly" ("Jesus is calling for you and for me"); or the evocative "Let the Lower Lights Be Burning" by Philip Bliss—the words we sing at the close of each night's sing at Rockbound Chapel, on our hill over the sea. Bliss, who joined the evangelistic team of Dwight Moody and Ira Sankey in 1869, envisioned Jesus as the lighthouse and His followers as points of light along the shore, saving those in peril: "Let the lower lights be burning! Send a gleam across the wave: some poor fainting, struggling seaman you may rescue, you may save." It's our house hymn. At the end of our singing, we may hear the waves on the shore, and often the moon and stars shine down on us as we leave the chapel, still humming the tune.

Our encyclopedia would include hymns of blessing like "We Gather Together," sung at many Thanksgiving Day tables—a hymn of unknown Dutch origin composed at the end of the seventeenth century. Originally, this was not recited in gratitude for the harvest but for the victory of the Dutch Protestants over their Spanish rulers and the domination of the Catholic Church: "The wicked oppressing now cease from distressing; sing praises to His name—He forgets not His own." It has evolved into a hymn of thanks rather than a generic war song, a category I purposely avoid here. (Think about "Onward Christian Soldiers" and others that dress Jesus in full armor and put Him in a tank.)

Our joy encyclopedia would certainly encompass the great slave spirituals, too many to list here, like "We Are Climbing Jacob's Ladder," source unknown ("we are climbing higher, higher, we are climbing higher, higher"), and "Were You There?" again, source unknown ("Were you there when they crucified my Lord? Were you there when they nailed Him to the tree?"), again, a song like "The Old Rugged Cross" that places us at the site, at the time.

My book would include hymns of tranquillity like Katherine von Schlegel's mid-eighteenth-century "Be Still My Soul," set to the music of Jean Sibelius's *Finlandia,* or Horatio Spafford's (1828–88) "It Is Well With My Soul," composed in deep depression after his four daughters were drowned in a shipwreck. "When peace like river, attendeth my way, when sorrow like sea billows roll; Whatever my lot, Thou hast taught me to say, It is well, it is well with my soul."

Dozens of great hymns about peace would be found in our encyclopedia: "Blest Be the Ties That Bind" by John Fawcett (1740–1817), sung by our tiny Long Island church congregation as we hold hands in a circle following monthly communion serv-ice—an immensely moving moment—or "In Christ There Is No East or West" by John Oxenham (1851–1941): "In Christ there is no East or West, in Him no South or North, But one great fel-lowship of love thruout the whole wide earth."

And there would be songs that celebrate the act of singing itself: Fanny Crosby's "Blessed Assurance" with its stirring chorus, "This is my story, this is my song, praising my Savior all the day long"; or Catherine Hankey's (1834–1911) "I Love to Tell the Story" ("of unseen things above"); or Philip Bliss's (1838–1876) "Wonderful Words of Life" ("Sing them over again to me, wonderful words of life"); or the snappy "In My Heart There Rings a Melody," words and music by Elton Roth (1891–1951), a Texas preacher who was suddenly inspired and wrote his song in a few minutes. "In my heart there rings a melody, there rings a melody of love."

And our giant book would list many hymns of faith like Frederick Faber's (1814–63) "Faith of Our Fathers" ("living still, in spite of dungeon, fire and sword"), and Isaac Watts's "Oh God Our Help in Ages Past," a paraphrase of Psalm 90, and one of his finest compositions.

Our faith hymns would include Thomas Chisholm's (1866–1960) wonderfully singable "Living for Jesus" ("Living for Jesus, a life that is true") and Folliott Pierpoint's (1835–1917) "For the Beauty of the Earth" ("for the joy of human love . . . for the Church . . . we raise this our hymn of grateful praise").

Several of the grand old songs that comfort us at death must be listed here: "Nearer My God to Thee" by Sarah Flower Adams (1805–48), a Unitarian composition that succeeds because it omits the evangelical fervor of lesser efforts, always remembered as the song played by the ship's band in 1912 as the *Titanic* went down.

I'd also appreciate Thomas A. Dorsey's (1899–1993) "Precious Lord, Take My Hand" ("lead me home") and Annie S. Hawks's (1835–1918) "I Need Thee Every Hour" ("I need Thee, O I need Thee"), a poem composed in a moment of inspiration in 1872 by this thirty-seven-year-old wife and mother.

And finally for comfort, I would call upon Civilla D. Martin's (1869–1948) "His Eye Is on the Sparrow" based on Matthew 10:29–31, "Not a sparrow falls to the ground without the will of your Father." I love the rousing change-of-pace refrain: "I sing because I'm happy, I sing because I'm free, for His eye is on the sparrow, and I know He watches me" (I hit the word "free" with gusto).

Above all, ours is a religion of love. I have discussed many of our love songs in the preceding pages, but I must also list Joseph Scriven's (1819–86) "What a Friend We Have in Jesus," and Charles Wesley's (1707–88) "Love Divine, All Loves Excelling" with its powerful final line, "Lost in wonder, love and praise," and George Matheson's (1842–1902) "Oh Love That Will Not Let Me Go," a song that came upon this blind Scottish minister like "a dayspring from on high"; and Cecil F. Alexander's (1818–95) "Jesus Calls Us" ("Jesus calls us from the worship of the vain world's golden store, from each idol that would keep us, saying 'Christian, love me more'").

And so very many others.

When I started this book, I realized that in no way could I ever include all of the grand old songs. I wrote a note to myself: "This book is impossible. That's why I'm going to do it."

I have selected the songs that touch me. But there is so much more to sing about.

And, of course, singing is not what's ultimately important. We have to live the songs we sing, and that is the real challenge. Like the Shakers we must walk through each day singing in our hearts or voices and trying to live the words we sing. If this is not the case, it is better that we remain mute.

ACKNOWLEDGMENTS

I am deeply grateful for early advice and encouragement from Genie and Lily Henderson and also from my editor, Martin Beiser, and my agent, Eric Simonoff. Also thanks to Jon Galassi, Doris Grumbach, Rev. Alice Hildebrand, Rev. Rob McCall, Pat Strachan, Paul Sullivan, Hannah Turner, Kirby Williams, Richard Wyatt, and to Rev. George Wilson, who, after I had been long outside of the church, showed me the way back in.

SELECT BIBLIOGRAPHY

Andrews, Edward D. *The Gift to Be Simple* (New York: Dover, 1962).

Bull, Josiah. *John Newton of Olney and St. Mary Wollnoth* (London: Religious Tract Society, 1868).

Campion, Nardi Reeder. *Mother Ann Lee* (Hanover, N.H.: University Press of New England, 1976).

Cecil, Richard. *The Life of John Newton,* ed. Marylynn Rouse (Fearn, Ross-shire: Christian Focus Publications, 2000).

Collins, Judy. *Amazing Grace* (New York, Hyperion, 1991).

Epstein, Dena J. *Sinful Tunes and Spirituals* (Urbana, Ill.: University of Illinois Press, 1977).

Green, Julien. *God's Fool* (New York: Harper & Row, 1985).

Habig, Marion, ed. *St. Francis of Assisi, Writings and Early Biographies,* Vols. I and II (Quincy, Ill.: Franciscan Press, 1991).

Heilbut, Tony. *The Gospel Sound: Good News and Bad Times* (New York: Simon & Schuster, 1971).

James, William. *The Varieties of Religious Experience* (New York: Penguin, 1982).

Jones, Arthur C. *Wade in the Water* (Maryknoll, N.Y.: Orbis Books, 1993).

Le Goff, Jacques. *St. Francis of Assisi* (London: Routledge, 2004).

Martin, Bernard. *John Newton: A Biography* (London: Heinemann, 1950).

Martin, Valerie. *Salvation* (New York: Vintage, 2002).

Marty, Martin. *Martin Luther* (New York: Viking, 2004).

McKim, LindaJo, ed. *The Presbyterian Hymnal* (Louisville: Westminster/John Knox Press, 1990).

Osbeck, Kenneth W. *Amazing Grace* (Grand Rapids: Kregel, 1990).

Patterson, Daniel W. *The Shaker Spiritual* (Mineola, N.Y.: Dover, 2000).

Pollock, John. *Amazing Grace: The Life of John Newton* (London: Hodder & Stoughton, 1981).

Turner, Steve. *Amazing Grace* (New York: Ecco, 2002).

INDEX

ABOUT THE AUTHOR

BILL HENDERSON is founder and editor of the acclaimed Pushcart Prize series, which each year selects from thousands of nominations the best fiction, essays, and poetry from small presses and little magazines for publication in an annual anthology. Before starting Pushcart Press in 1972, he worked as an editor at Doubleday and Putnam. He has taught at Princeton and Columbia and has been a guest lecturer at Johns Hopkins, Sarah Lawrence, and Radcliffe. He has published three memoirs—*Tower* (Farrar, Straus and Giroux), *Her Father* (Faber and Faber), and *His Son* (W.W. Norton)—and is an elder in the Springs Community Presbyterian Church, Long Island.

He and his wife and daughter divide their time between East Hampton, New York and Down East Maine.

Simple Gifts

ONE MAN'S SEARCH

FOR GRACE

BILL HENDERSON

ABOUT THIS INTERVIEW

The following author interview is intended to help you find an interesting and rewarding approach to your reading of *Simple Gifts*. We hope this enhances your enjoyment and appreciation of the book.

Questions for Bill Henderson

What made you decide to write this book?

Writing teachers often dictate, "Write about what you know." I think it is more important that we write about what moves us deeply. When I found myself weeping unexpectedly while singing certain hymns, I had to know what was in these hymns that meant so much to me and to the others I was singing with. There is a deep source here. I wrote to find that source and to tell others what I had discovered.

Are you vocal about your beliefs?

In person I try to act like the Christian I am trying to become. (I don't think one can say, "I am a Christian." It's always a becoming, a progress that is never complete.) At our little church on Long Island we sing a sending hymn: "Go now and in love; show you believe, reach out to others, so all the world can see." That's my idea of testifying, reaching out to others in both large and small ways, enlarging the community of love. It's easy to announce, "I am a Christian"; plenty of scoundrels have done that.

Vision . . . daughter . . . other experiences?

My epiphany of love infusing the universe when my daughter was injured has never been repeated. It was one time, and it was overwhelming. The world was on fire with love in that episode. But many smaller events have increased my faith and made me aware of our surrounding mystery. For instance, the presence that filled the room during chemo treatments—an undeniable force. I am convinced we are not alone. Most often I know this when others are sharing love and joy. The world is whole then. It's quite apparent what the truth is. Love is simply the way God works.

Favorite memories of singing in church?

I have hundreds of wonderful memories of singing in church, and I always feel deeply connected to my fellow singers. *Simple Gifts* includes many such hymns and occasions. Only bad hymns (lousy lyrics, impossible-to-sing music) drive me down and separate the congregation into ill-humored atoms. Poor hymns, like dull sermons, are bad for the spirit.

Favorite hymn recording?

Paul Robeson singing "Balm In Gilead," Mahalia Jackson's rendition of "His Eye Is On the Sparrow," and very precious to me is the Westover School's DVD of the girls (my daughter among them) singing "In the Bleak Midwinter." But my favorite hymn recording is a video, *Amazing Grace,* the Bill Moyers document. In it all the myriad renditions of that hymn are explored and represented, from ordinary folks singing shape notes to the legendary diva Jessye Norman, recalling her childhood and singing the hymn to Moyers backstage. *Amazing Grace* also happens to be my favorite hymn, but I love so many more.

Secular music?

I love all sorts of music, but I am most profoundly moved by classical works by Chopin, Beethoven, and Prokofiev. Their music got me though chemo, particularly Prokofiev's ironic and frolicking symphonies. Paul Winter's annual winter solstice concert at St. John the Divine Cathedral in New York is especially important to me, as are the delicate impressions of Maine composer and pianist Paul Sullivan.

Influence of parents?

My parents were both rock-steady, decent, kind, and responsible. They poured all of their love and energy into raising my brother, sister, and myself during difficult times—the end of the Depression, World War II, the Cold War, and periods of economic insecurity when my father was sure he was going to lose his job. My mother went back to work as a high school math teacher to enable us to afford college. Their church was everything to them, and even if I don't agree with their limited interpretations of Christianity—particularly my father's—I owe them deeply. When my daughter was born, parenting came easily to me. I had been well taught in the basics by my own parents. Their joy in their children become my joy in my daughter, and I know that now that she is grown, her own children in the future will benefit from what my parents taught me.

Life changes after surviving cancer?

I don't know for sure that I have survived. So far, so good. But I now know in hard reality how very rare and sacred life is. That we all die one day is no longer just an idea; it became very real to me while I was undergoing chemotherapy, radiation, and three operations. I also learned that "me" is not very important. It's not about me. At times I was depressed, angry, and felt betrayed by my affection for religion. "A fraud," I thought, while chemically exhausted, but that's ridiculous, I now know. I am a small part of a very great mystery, and I am very grateful for that part as long as I may live. I found spiritual and physical reserves I never knew I had.

What does the experience of writing mean to you?

As I said earlier, I write about what moves me profoundly. My first memoir, *His Son,* is about my silent dad and my attempt to know him better after he died. My second memoir, *Her Father,* is about the birth of my daughter after my misspent Manhattan years, and how the miracle of her birth and the love of my wife led me back to the love of the little church down the road. My memoir, *Tower,* is about a compulsion to build a tower on a hill in Maine during a period of spiritual depression, and how building that tower revived my soul. All the memoirs chronicle an estrangement from the church and a returning. They are about loss of faith and its constant resurgence. Now I write for God, the reader, and love—my love letters to the world that I call my memoirs. To have a story published in *Esquire* or to be lionized for a great American novel (whatever that is) seems just silly.

What are you working on now? What is most satisfying?

My most satisfying project is always the one I am working on now. At the moment that project is a memoir about building a stone chapel in the Maine woods over a period of five years, stone by stone hauled from the fields and local abandoned quarries. The chapel is plain, simple, and rough. I anchored it to a granite ledge deep in the woods, and I hope it is a reminder of the endurance of faith.

What is Pushcart Press?

When I started Pushcart in 1972, I was a soon-to-be ex-editor at Doubleday, then a giant in the commercial publishing industry, now a mere shell of its former self. I found commercial publishing to be, well, commercial, and therefore about money mostly, and rather boring. Pushcart's first book, published from a tiny studio apartment in Yonkers, New York, was *The Publish Yourself Handbook,* which attempted to convince authors that they didn't absolutely need commercial or vanity publishers. All they required was their own moxie. It sold 70,000 copies over the years and helped spark the modern small press movement.

The annual *Pushcart Prize: Best of the Small Presses* was first published in 1976 with the backing of many distinguished founding editors: Paul Bowles, Ralph Ellison, Joyce Carol Oates, Reynolds Price, and Anaïs Nin among them. Over the past three decades we've honored the poetry, stories, and essays of thousands of writers as selected from hundreds of small presses and little magazines.

The publishing landscape has become even more commercial than it was in the 1970s, making small presses even more important, particularly for poetry essays and short stories. Pushcart's role hasn't changed much over the years. Now I publish from a shack in my Long Island backyard with a telephone and typewriter and lots of help. Pushcart continues as a secretary and cheerleader for the literary underground.

Balancing work between editor and writer?

In the summer and fall I am mostly a writer, although I find it impossible to write in the July heat. In the winter and spring I am a Pushcart Prize reader and editor. Both jobs are immensely gratifying to me.

Writers who have influenced you the most?

Two books by Reynolds Price are particularly important to me: *A Palpable God* and *A Whole New Life*. I'd recommend anything by Wendell Berry, including his poems. He is a soul mate although I have never met him. Flannery O'Connor is close to my heart. I've read all of her short stories and novels, and in one week I devoured all six hundred pages of her collected letters, *The Habit of Being*. I've listed many books in my bibliography in *Simple Gifts* that have helped me, and I'd like to recommend the work of Michael S. Hamilton in *Christianity Today* on contemporary praise songs (July 17, 1999). My list of favorite authors is very long, and many seem to have religious views near to mine. They include: Peter Gomes, (*The Good Book*), Kathleen Norris, Alan Watts, Fyodor Dostoyevsky, Thich Nhat Hanh, Dan Wakefield (*Returning*), Doris Grumbach, James Carroll (*Constantine's Sword*), Marcus J. Borg, Georges Bernanos (especially *The Diary of a Country Priest*), Garry Wills, A. N. Wilson, Steven Mitchell, John Dominic Crossan, Leo Tolstoy (particularly *Resurrection* and the later works), Paul Johnson (*A History of Christianity*), St. Augustine, and Elaine Pagels. In the Bible I am most encouraged by the Gospels of Mark, Matthew, and Luke, plus Paul's letters.

Advice for readers of this book?

We must realize that organized religion is a narrative built on the divine example of Jesus. It is a very human narrative, corrupted by all very human sins, lust for power, secular political maneuvering, shading of truth for personal advantage, committee politics, outright lies. I see Christianity as the perfect pearl of Jesus encrusted with much that is false and compromised. At the center always for me is Jesus. People crucify him again and again every day by misusing his name to justify sexism, racism, war, even torture and other horrors. It has been this way though history, but for me that does not destroy the sacred message at the center. Remember this: There is no contradiction in Jesus' message of infinite compassion.

What brings you joy?

Conversations and laughter with good friends, walking my gamboling dogs on the beach, a sunrise over the Maine ocean, likewise a moonrise; a brilliant red cardinal singing on a dull winter day, the taste of fresh peas from my garden—the list of my favorite things is almost endless. We are surrounded by miracle and wonder.

CREDITS